Lorraine,
Keep your entrepreneurial dreams alive, get your marketing into ACTION and continually strive to become a #SmallBizMarketingGu

Small Business Marketing Made EZ!

By Stacey Riska,

The Small Biz Marketing Specialist

Small Business Marketing Made EZ!

Published by Small Business Expertise Publishing
10319 Westlake Drive
#105
Bethesda, MD 20817

Printed in the United States of America.

ISBN: 978-1-7322459-0-7

Cover design by Jim Saurbaugh

DISCLAIMER AND/OR LEGAL NOTICES

While the publisher and authors have used their best efforts in preparing this book, they make no representations or warranties with respect to the accuracy or completeness of the contents of this book. The advice and strategies contained herein may not be suitable for your situation. You should consult a professional where appropriate. Neither the publisher nor the authors shall be liable for any loss of profit or any other commercial damages, including but not limited to special, incidental, consequential, or other damages. The purchaser or reader of this publication assumes responsibility for the use of these materials and information. Adherence to all applicable laws and regulations, both advertising and all other aspects of

To "Digital Dave," my business partner, my husband, my best friend

Table of Contents

Foreword

Over the years, I've met a lot of people who proclaim to be "small business experts." In my opinion, the ones most worth listening to built their "expertise" in the trenches while running their own small businesses. Their valuable expertise comes directly from experiencing the highs and lows of running a business and the realization that while hard work is mandatory, tapping into others for help is often needed to find the path to success. These are the people who have great advice and are willing to pay it forward by sharing it with others. As you'll see in Stacey's incredible story, her advice is based on her real-life experiences in riding some massive business rollercoasters, getting inspiration and help along the way from others, and then paying it forward on a daily basis and through this incredible book.

One of the wonderful things about running Alignable is being able to provide people like Stacey with a frictionless way to share her insights and ideas with business owners across North America. While she regularly shares advice on a broad range of topics, she's most recognized for the incredible insights she provides about the vital role marketing plays in business success.

Marketing is the secret weapon for small business success.

Secret because small business owners don't really like talking about marketing challenges with others. "I really not a marketing expert."

Weapon because when done right, it holds the power to dramatically increase your likelihood of success.

Why is marketing so critical for success? Because you need customers to succeed, and marketing is all about bringing the right ones (the ones who want what you have to offer) through your front door.

There are two ways to get in front of these people:

1. Use your passion and expertise to build a network of people willing to recommend you to others.
2. Pay someone to reach your customer demographic to get you in front of them.

I've spent the last 15 years building software applications that focus on #1 because I believe it's the part that lends itself to the competitive advantage of being a small business owner: personal connection with customers and others willing to put their reputation on the line for you and your business. This thesis is supported by a recent survey we conducted in which over 7,000 small business owners shared their best source for new customer acquisition. The result? Eighty-five percent selected word-of-mouth referrals. That's not to say #2 (paid advertising) isn't important to understand and leverage when you have the resources to do so. However, in my opinion, you can't truly succeed without mastering #1.

Whether you're just getting started or in the midst of the rollercoaster finding your way, this book will help you drive toward greater success.

Eric Groves
Co-Founder & CEO
Alignable.com
The Small Business Network

This Is Not a Book

You may not realize it yet, but you're not holding a book, whether what you're holding is in print or digital form. That's right! This is ***not*** a book. What you're actually holding is a key. In fact, it's ***the*** key to everything you always envisioned your small business would be. If you're like most entrepreneurs, you launched your business with lofty expectations and dreams. The reasons you started your business may vary, but no one launches a business with visions of failure.

Maybe you started your business because you have, or do, something so amazing that the world needs to know about it because it's the solution to a huge problem....

Maybe you started your business to provide a comfortable life for you and your family....

Maybe you started your business to fund your retirement...

Maybe you started your business to leave a legacy and have something to pass down to the next generation...

Maybe you started your business to have the freedom to live the life you always wanted, tired of working hard for someone else or in the corporate world, trading hours for dollars....

Maybe you started your business to achieve financial freedom, working when and where you want....

Whatever the reason, you started your business because you had no doubt you would be successful - otherwise you wouldn't have done it, right? Like I said, no one starts with visions of failure.

Well I have a question for you:

"Howz that working out for ya?"

> Any entrepreneur who launches a business does so to leverage their skills and knowledge and to gain personal and financial freedom. No one sets out to fail.

If you're anything like me and most other entrepreneurs, when you first launched your business, you had grandiose visions of the success you and your business would achieve. You would achieve complete financial freedom, earning more than you ever would working for someone else. You would work when and where you wanted - according to your own perfect schedule. You would secure a retirement filled with travel, your hobbies, and whatever your heart desired.

You never imagined that you'd work longer hours, being tied to your business day in and day out. You never imagined that turning a decent profit (let alone an enviable one) could be so difficult. You never in a million years would have thought your retirement could mean you'd be a greeter at Walmart just to make ends meet!

So why has it gone wrong for so many entrepreneurs? Why has it possibly gone so wrong for you? That's a great question that I will answer in this "not a book," but even better than that, I will share with you exactly how to achieve that vision you had the day you started your business - the one filled with personal and financial freedom. Whether you're a new business owner striving to reach the six-figure mark or a business that's doing "okay" but you want to reach seven figures and more, this super easy six-step business-building system is exactly what you've been waiting for - so keep reading!

Been There, Done That

My name is Stacey Riska, and I'm known internationally as "Small Business Stacey" because I eat, sleep, and breathe small business. I love helping businesses on Main Street and beyond thrive and create something much more than just a job. There are countless people who leave the traditional workplace and launch their businesses only to discover that they haven't created the enterprise they envisioned - filled with the time and financial freedom they want, they've simply created a new "job" for themselves... a job that will never fulfill their dreams.

My personal mission is to help 10,000 small business owners build million-dollar, profitable businesses, so they can live the life they've dreamed about and make all of the reasons they started their business a reality. And that includes funding a handsome retirement because I'm quite sure nobody's dream is to eat Ramen noodles in their twilight years!

I'm not some guru preaching from the mountain top to take the steps needed to be a successful entrepreneur who's never done it themselves, and I don't live in an ivory tower. I'm just like you - a small business owner who gets up every day with a goal of increasing my bank account, providing for my family, saving for retirement, leaving a legacy, and living the life I always wanted.

> I've been where you are... so yeah, "Been there, done that." But I learned how to turn it around and achieve great success.

I "get" what it's like to be in the trenches every day. I "get" what it's like to not know if you're going to be able to make payroll. I "get" what it's like to feel frustrated that the clients and accounts aren't coming in. That's why I'm so passionate about helping small business owners. That's why I'm so passionate about helping you!

Today, I'm in a much different place than I was just a few years ago. Like I said, I'm just like you, so let me share a very brief synopsis of my back story:

My first dive into entrepreneurship was about 20 years ago. I started a business doing the back office work for associations and non-profits: data entry, call centers, mailing, and fulfillment. I loved it because it was "hands on" and I got to do the work. After ten years of growing a successful and profitable business, I had two amazing project managers running the show, and I wasn't so involved in the day-to-day operations. It was then that I "had my midlife crisis" and decided I needed something "fun" to do. I was ready for a change.

So… I bought a coffee and smoothie franchise. Makes sense, right? After all, what could be more fun than standing behind a tiki bar, wearing a bright Hawaiian shirt, saying "Aloha!" and serving umbrella drinks? It was my dream job or at the very least, it was my dream job of something fun… something different… something that would allow me to be my own boss.

By the end of my second year in business, I was the #1 franchisee in the system. I had ten mobile tiki bars in operation as well as two stores at Dulles International Airport outside of Washington D.C. and one store in a mall. The growth was great. But then, so was the crash and burn! My crash and burn occurred in 2008 when the economy tanked and it seemed everything fell apart. No one was going out to the mall just to get a smoothie. I had a ton of overhead and expense wrapped up in the mall location. No one was traveling, so no one was visiting either of my kiosks at the airport where I had twice as much overhead and fixed expense as at the mall. Everyone was in belt-tightening mode, worried about their own job security and watching every penny. No one was spending money on anything that wasn't absolutely necessary. I assure you, smoothies from the tiki bar, despite the cute little umbrella and despite being served with a now strained smile and "Aloha" don't garner much, if any, disposable income.

I was $500,000 in debt, and I didn't know where my next customer was coming from. I was so broke I didn't even have enough money to buy the next week's inventory. I was working 100+ hours a week, exhausting myself because I was working "in" the business, not "on" the business. My family didn't get any of my time or attention. My kids didn't have their mom there to help with homework, go to activities, or be there for them just to ask, "How was your day?" My husband, who had started in the business with me, was forced to take a job he despised just to keep our family afloat. The house was a disaster. There was rarely a good home-cooked meal to eat. Those were very dire times, and I really almost lost it all - my home, my family, even my life.

It's a subject I tear up about every time I tell the story because it was so real and frighteningly difficult.

If my story were to be a movie, it would include every genre - drama, action, horror, comedy - all intertwined. I would have needed Jim Carey in *Fun with Dick and Jane* to represent the comedic side of how everything went downhill. I would have needed Bruce Willis in any of the *Die Hard* movies to represent the "action" of daily battles being fought and things "blowing up." I would have needed to combine *The Godfather* with *Parenthood* to illustrate what a dysfunctional house I had. And ultimately I would have needed Sylvester Stallone in all of the *Rocky* movies to represent the beating I took on a daily basis.

I'll never forget the day I had my "finding Jesus" moment. I was driving home from working yet another 14-hour day, and I just started crying. But not just crying… I mean bawling so hard my chest was heaving. I couldn't breathe, and it was so bad I had to pull over on the side of the road. I remember it took a good five minutes before I "came through," and I know it sounds so clichéd, but this is absolutely true. I listened to what was playing on the radio, and it was Kelly Clarkson singing "What doesn't kill you makes you stronger. " I started laughing at that moment and said, "Stacey, this is your new theme song."

I knew at that moment I was at that proverbial "fork in the road." I had a big decision to make and it came down to two choices: Throw in the towel, close down the business, and figure out how to pay back $500,000 in debt (very likely losing my home in the process) or fight to save my business and make it work.

I decided to fight because I knew that I had a viable business that could and should be making money. Sure, it was easy to blame the failure on the economy, but ultimately it was me - and what I was ***not*** doing - that had put my business in the difficult and precarious position it was in.

I did figure it out. I was able to save my business. But not only did I save it, I took it from $500,000 in debt to becoming a seven-figure profitable business. When I realized how easy it was to create this turn-around and to make my business become what I'd envisioned and dreamed about, I became really passionate about helping other small business owners do the same thing, so they could have similar results. That's why today I run the Small Biz Marketing Specialist - a done-for-you marketing agency that helps every small business owner become a #SmallBizMarketingWiz and get their marketing ***done***.

The question I'm always asked (and the one you're probably wondering right now) is: "How did you go from $500,000 in debt to a seven-figure profitable business?"

The answer is one word.

One word that changed it all for me.

One word that allowed me to have the type of business along with the personal and financial freedom that I wanted.

One word that has enabled me to look ahead to the retirement I desire.

One word that can change it all for you, too.

One word that can allow you to create exactly the type of business ***you*** want.

One word that will allow you to work on your business rather than in your business.

So, what is this one word?

Marketing.

Marketing is the magic word. Marketing is the thing that every small business owner knows they need to do, yet so many struggle with it. Sure there are the excuses: "I don't have time." "I don't have the expertise." "I'm not a marketer."

> Marketing is the cornerstone of your success, and marketing does not have to complicated or difficult… quite the opposite.

Phooey!

If you've said or even thought any of those things, I'm here to tell you you're wrong. I'm here to tell you marketing is easy and you ***can*** do it. And you can do it in six simple steps. I'm going to show you exactly what to do and how to do it. These same simple steps are what I used to transform my coffee and smoothie business. They are also the same steps I now use to help my clients grow their businesses.

This is not a book that you'll read and then put on the shelf. This is a book that becomes an active part of your business. In these pages, I will walk you through creating the marketing plan you'll follow and implement to build a successful and profitable business. If you've been looking for a no-nonsense way to stand out and rise above your competition so you can sell more of what it is you sell with less stress and more predictability and profit, without busting your bank account, you're in the right place.

This book is for you – the small business owner – whether on Main Street or beyond who wants ***more***:

- ***more*** leads
- ***more*** customers
- ***more*** clients
- ***more*** patients
- ***more*** sales
- and ***more*** money!

It's your roadmap to creating business stability, financial peace of mind, and more freedom to do what you want because it gives you the tools and strategies you need to elevate you above your competition both next door and online. It's your blueprint with the step-by-step instructions to grow a successful and profitable business that you love (again). You can do it.

Ready to get started?

To your business success,

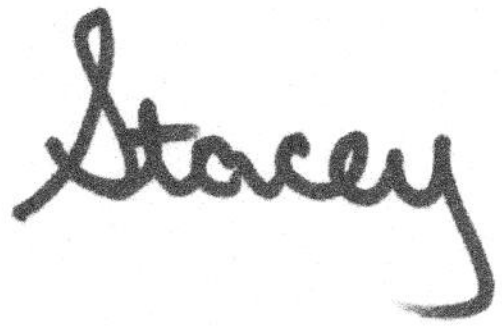

"Small Business Stacey"
#SmallBizMarketingWiz

Chapter One:

Let's Get Rid of the Excuses

Perhaps you've heard the statistic: Nine out of ten small businesses fail within ten years. Other stats are equally frightening and dismal. About 20 percent never make it past their first year. Half are gone by their fifth year.

Do you want to be one these statistics? Are you on the path to becoming one right now? Did you launch your business to fail?

I can remember the first time I heard that 96 percent of businesses fail in ten years. I was shocked and upset. How can this be? Most people are smart, and if they have taken the risk to go out on their own and start their own companies, they are willing to take calculated risks. Small businesses are part of the American Dream. It's how entrepreneurs control their own destiny and make the world a better place. Small business is one of the real economic drivers in the country. Small businesses employ the more than half of all U.S. workers.

But how can that happen if only four out of 100 businesses survive past the ten-year mark? If your company is a decade or more old, then congratulations - you're one of the four percent and in elite company! If your business is less than 10 years old, then I would like to share one of the most important lessons I learned from my mentor, friend, and business coach, Jim Palmer. "You need to have a GPS to build your dream business - Guts, Persistence and Strategy." This could be the defining difference between going out of business and accomplishing the very goals you set out to achieve.

If you ask these nine out of ten small business owners why they went out of business, most will tell you "they ran out of cash." I have seen countless reports that state that the reason small businesses fail so quickly is a problem with cash flow. I disagree! If businesses were profitable and making money, cash flow would be significantly less of an issue. Where cash flow could become an issue is in the exact opposite scenario - fast growth. My guess is you're not reading this book if you're in that position.

> Businesses don't fail because of a lack of cash flow; businesses fail because of a lack of marketing.

Alignable, a free network where small business owners build trusted relationships and generate referrals, did a survey of small business owners asking, "What is the #1 challenge you struggle with?"

How do you think they answered? Operations? Finances/Accounting? Technology?

None of those. The #1 challenge small business owners say they struggle with is marketing.

The primary reason small businesses fail is because they don't do marketing or they don't do it correctly. It's that plain and simple. No marketing equals no business growth. No business growth leads you to becoming one of those scary statistics.

Every small business owner will tell you they ***know*** they need to market to grow their business. They know it can be the difference maker when it comes to bringing more customers, clients, or patients in the door. Yet they don't do it. They make excuses why they aren't doing it.

Here are the top ten excuses I hear why small business owners do not do marketing.

1. There's Just Not Enough Time

Business owners say they don't have enough time to focus on marketing. Let's face it. As a business owner is there ***ever*** enough time for anything? If marketing were the #1 thing you could do to save your business, would you make the time? Or find someone who can do it for you?

2. I'm Already Doing Other Things

Running a business means wearing a lot of hats. Sure, you're the CEO - Chief Everything Officer. You're busy keeping customers happy and offering the products and services they need. Yes, those mainstays of running a business are definitely important. You could be the best tutor, dog walker, or day care owner in the world, but your services aren't going to sell themselves if nobody knows about them.

3. I'm Not Clever Enough for Marketing

Even if you're not the type of person who has ideas popping into your head all day, there are ways to develop marketing campaign ideas. Things you already do, based on events, seasons, and time of year, provide a great starting point for generating marketing ideas.

4. I Don't Know Anything about Marketing

You don't have to. The good news about marketing is there are plenty of simple ways to get started, from using social media to sending out emails or creating content to help your customers, clients, or patients. To take your business to the next level, you might even consider outsourcing. A marketing agency can help you with one-off projects such as designing your website to managing all of your day-to-day marketing activities. Yes, it will cost you a little money but in the long run will be worth it. You will get a return on what you spend when you choose the right company. My motto has always been, "Do what you do best, outsource the rest."

5. I Don't Have the Budget

That's what everyone says. There are many no- and low-cost ways to do marketing that will return strong results.

6. It's Too Complicated

With what seems like a new tool, tip, and technology coming out every day with a lingo all its own, yes, it can seem very complicated and overwhelming. But just because it's the newest, latest, and greatest doesn't mean it's the best. Especially for your small business. Do a few simple things well. Lather, rinse, repeat. Not complicated at all.

7. I Have Enough Customers

When business owners have business coming in, they don't think they need to be marketing. But they're wrong. Being proactive about growing your business is critical to your long-term success. If you wait until you ***need*** customers, clients, or patients, you've waited too long!

8. Marketing Doesn't Work

Some small business owners throw an ad in the paper, post something on social media, or put up a website. When they don't get any response, they say, "Marketing doesn't work." That's like saying, "I put gas in my car, but it's not moving."

9. Everyone Already Knows About Us

Do they really? Are you sure? While you most certainly have your core customers, what about people new to the area who may be looking for just what you have to offer? Or someone who has been going to a competitor for years, had a bad experience, and is now looking to make a change?

10. I Can't Keep Up with It All

It's true. There are a lot of choices out there. Online marketing, offline marketing. SEO, SEM, PPC, CMS, CTR - acronyms you hadn't heard of before. Digital marketing is changing every day, but that doesn't mean you need to be overwhelmed by it nor become an expert in it. Let the other guys figure it out and make the mistakes.

How many of those ten excuses do you tell yourself every day? Let's squash them now. Get a piece of paper and write down what's been holding you back from getting your marketing done. Seriously, do it right now. I'll wait....

> Dispense with every excuse you ever uttered about why you're not getting your marketing done. Not one of them holds water, and no excuse will get you results.

Now crumble that piece of paper into a tight ball and throw it in the trash. It is the last time you will ever have an excuse because this book - this key to your success - is going to make getting your marketing done EZ.

With your list now in the trash, congrats! You're starting with a clean slate. You no longer have any excuses. You're ready to start marketing. However, the problem is that without having a clear marketing plan of what to do, when, and how to do it, you'll fall into one of the following four "approaches to marketing."

Spaghetti Marketing

Can you guess what spaghetti marketing is? A lot of small businesses do it. Maybe you've tried it as well.

Simply spend a lot of marketing dollars randomly, throw a bunch of "spaghetti" against the wall, and see if anything sticks.

Here's a dialogue of how it happens:

"Today I'm going to try email marketing. After all, it's free.

"Well that didn't work. No one responded.

"Forget email marketing - it doesn't work. Instead, I'm going to post some things on social media. I bet that will work. After all, everyone is on social media.

"Gosh, that didn't work either. Maybe I'll run some Facebook ads instead. After all, I've heard so many people are making millions. Just set up an ad, people will "like" me, and leads will come in.

"I spent ***that*** much and didn't get any business? Not even a few measly leads? Social media marketing is just for the big guys.

"Let me post some content on my blog. Some guru said, 'Content is king,' and I should be doing content marketing.

"Well that didn't generate any leads either.
"This marketing stuff doesn't work!"

Spaghetti marketing happens because the small business owner has good intentions, and they want to get quick results. So they're doing things fast - a "one-and-done" approach. They'll try something once, see that it doesn't provide ***immediate*** results, so they try something else - throwing more spaghetti at the wall, hoping something eventually sticks. There's no strategy behind it; it's all random. "Let's try this," and "Let's try that." When nothing happens - at least based on their expectations - they quickly move on to the "next shiny object." It's an ineffective, and many times, expensive way to approach marketing.

Spaghetti marketers stay very busy, but they are not as productive or profitable as they know they can and should be. You'll find them constantly on social media, creating but never seeing results.

You know that you've been spaghetti marketing when you're doing "a lot of things" but have nothing to show for it.

As you might suspect, I am not a big fan of spaghetti marketing. You could throw a lot of spaghetti – actually your hard-earned money – against the wall before you ever get anything to stick. There's no guarantee that anything will stick, or if it does, for how long.

Perfectionism Marketing

You are proud of your business. You want to make an amazing impression on everyone - your prospects, your leads, your customers, clients, or patients. You want everything to be perfect.

Perfectionism is the all-or-nothing attitude that sounds like this:

- "I put together a marketing campaign, but I'm not sure it's ready to roll out yet. It's not quite perfect."
- "I'm not going to send this out yet. It needs to look more professional."
- "I can't do video. What if I goof up?"

You may say you don't want to put anything out unless it "looks professional" or is "professionally created." There is absolutely nothing wrong with things looking professional if they can be done in a realistic time frame. There is nothing wrong with working with a professional to create your marketing, as long as you don't cause "said professional" to age 12 years because of all of your "small edits." If you can't get something out because you are waiting on your web designer to return the 87th version of a basic five-page site, you need therapy… and now the poor web designer does, too!

This sort of perfectionism stimulates stress, crushes creativity, prevents productivity, and ultimately prunes profitability.

Most perfectionists don't even realize they are one. They cling to the belief that their obsessive pursuit of perfection is really just the definition of doing a good job. Yet perfectionism may be what is ultimately restricting them - and you - from desired success.

You know you struggle with perfectionism marketing if you find yourself:

- Editing social media posts again and again… and again.
- Writing but not posting blog content because the post isn't good enough.
- Obsessing over a website design and delaying edits until everything is "just right."
- Not trusting others to help with marketing.

Look, your marketing is never going to be perfect. You've got to let that perfectionist sh*t go. Inhale, exhale. Stop stressing. It's not worth it. Your success is not going to hinge on a single blog, social media post, or having the most beautiful web site.

Let's break down marketing perfectionism: Perfectionism is an unhealthy state of marketing that comes from a fear of failure. Of not being good enough. It limits your creativity and puts you in a tight box. It doesn't help your marketing and more importantly, does nothing to boost your creativity.

Great things happen when you let yourself be in the moment.

To get out of perfectionism marketing, you need to say, "Good is good enough." And I'm here to tell you it is. If you made a typo in your email and someone calls you out on it, great! They're reading. More importantly, they're initiating conversation. Truly, if all they have time to do is find faults with your marketing, they have ***way*** too much time on their hands and probably aren't a good customer, client, or patient anyway.

Ant Marketing

Have you ever seen a bunch of ants, all walking in a line, following each other? The ants in the back have no idea where they're really going. They're just following the ant in front of them, doing exactly what they're doing because if the ants ahead are doing it, they must be going in the right direction, right?

Ant marketing is the worst marketing of all. You think, "I'll do what everyone else is doing. After all, if they're doing something, it must be working, right?"

"Sally's Hair Salon sent out a coupon for 50% off, so I'll do that, too."

"Bob's Electric Service did a sponsorship and got a banner on the high school football field. I'm going do that, too."

"I see a lot of people posting stuff on social media, so I'll post even more than they do. Maybe then I'll be seen more."

Ant marketing is simply copying what everyone else is doing without having any thought or strategy behind it. As you might imagine, it can be very expensive and have dismal results.

Hopeless Marketing

This usually comes after trying all of the other approaches to marketing. After you've "thrown spaghetti at the wall" aka done lots of "things," after you slowed down and tried to perfect everything, after you tried to copy what everyone else is doing with ant marketing, you start to feel hopeless. You've done a lot of work for little or no reward. You've spent a lot of money (and time) with nothing to show for it. You consider trying a different strategy, but you doubt your abilities. You just want to give up on it. You feel stuck.

> Don't give up, and don't proclaim, "Marketing doesn't work." You simply need to know the best strategy and tactics for your small business.

You think about asking someone for marketing help, but you're not sure what that would look like.

You see only the cost of marketing because you haven't seen or don't believe in marketing's return on investment.

Your mantra is, "Marketing doesn't work," so you don't do any.

With hopeless marketing you feel like a loner on an island all by yourself where no one is coming to save you.

It can even make you question the business you're in and whether you should continue.

The result of hopeless marketing is you put marketing on the back burner and find things to keep you busy because if you're busy, then business must be good, right? We all know how the story ends. It ends with business failure that contributes to the statistics that I shared in the beginning of this chapter. You'll contend that you'll fail because of cash flow (e.g., running out of money), and I'll still insist that the problem is a failure to market… that leads to you to close up shop.

Which of the four marketing approaches are you taking now?

A Systematic Approach

Let's face it. None of us can be great at everything when it comes to running our businesses. Sure, when we start out, we have to do it all because we're figuring it all out - the systems aren't in place yet. But in order to grow, you ***must*** get those systems in place so that you can focus your time and attention on growing your business. Systems allow you to work on your business rather than working in your business. Systems lead to truly being an entrepreneur rather than owning a business in which you have simply created a job for yourself.

Systems are very important in regard to successful marketing because successful marketing involves a strategy and a plan. First you create the strategy and then develop the plan to implement that strategy. Your system will execute your plan according to your strategy. You won't be a victim of spaghetti marketing because you have a forward-thinking strategy rather than throwing everything against the wall, hoping that something sticks and generates a return on your hard-earned marketing investment. When you have a plan in place, you can overcome perfectionism marketing because you've created a timeline for implementation. You've determined the best course of action for your company, so you aren't subject to ant marketing. Finally, there's hope!

You've got two choices when it comes to growing your business... where the marketing is getting done. You can either do it yourself or hire an employee (or employees) to do it for you, or you can find outside contractors. There are pros and cons to either approach.

First, if you do it yourself, you maintain total control. That may seem attractive on the surface; however, you must honestly assess your skill set. Have you already struggled with spaghetti, perfectionism, or ant marketing only to throw your hands up and declare it all hopeless? When you're starting out, you can learn - in fact, you can employ the steps I'm going to cover in this book - but you must always keep in mind that the cost to you will be your time. Only you can determine where your time is best spent.

You can hire an employee to handle this critical function. The average cost to hire a full-time marketing director today is $120K. My guess is you don't have the resources to do that. Perhaps even hiring someone at half that salary is a stretch for your company. In addition, most small businesses don't need a full-time person, so maybe you'll pass off the duties to an existing employee. Chances are that person is not going to be an expert in all of the areas of marketing with which you'll want or need assistance. Someone who is great at social media is probably not an expert in direct mail. Someone who is great at graphic design is probably not great at reputation management.

Using outside resources to get your marketing done actually makes a lot of sense. Yet so few small business owners outsource their marketing. Why is that?

Consider these statistics: 54 percent of small businesses outsource graphic design and website design according to the 2017 WASP Barcode Technologies, "State of Small Business Report." But only 14 percent outsource their marketing, public relations, and advertising.

This comes up again in other studies. In the Infusionsoft 2017, "Small Business Marketing Trends Report," 70.8 percent of small businesses reported doing their marketing themselves.

So the overwhelming majority of small businesses choose to handle their marketing in-house, either by business owners doing it themselves or handing off the job to another employee. Unfortunately, this isn't working well. Street Fight's research on small business owners found that among business owners who either do their marketing themselves, delegate it to an internal team, or outsource it to an agency, the owners who do their marketing themselves are the least satisfied with their results.

> Focus on what you do best and outsource the rest!

The most satisfied? They're the owners who outsource marketing to an agency. (I'm willing to bet that these same owners also outsource their accounting, payroll, and tax preparation, so they can focus on their core competencies and growing their businesses!)

You've learned why so many small business owners struggle, especially when it comes to marketing. Knowledge is power. With what you've learned so far in this book, you can put the framework in place to ensure your marketing plan not only gets created - but gets done!

- Bye bye to gurus preaching stuff they've never done themselves.
- Bye bye to overwhelm of "too many things" to do in your business.
- Bye bye to the complexity of too many choices (social media ***alone*** offers more choices than most entrepreneurs can digest).
- Bye bye to wasting time and money trying to figuring out marketing.
- Bye bye to spaghetti marketing.
- Bye bye to perfectionism marketing.
- Bye bye to ant marketing.
- Bye bye to hopeless marketing.

It's time to start fresh and say hello to easy and effective marketing. It's time to say hello to getting it done! I'm going to show you how easy marketing is and the amazing results you can achieve. It's time to get into ACTION.

Get It Done the EZ Way:

- Plenty of small businesses fail, and most will chalk it up to cash flow; however, they fail because of poor, ineffective, or nonexistent marketing.
- There are plenty of excuses that entrepreneurs offer regarding their failure to market. I've heard them all, and they're just that - excuses.
- Spaghetti marketing - trying it all and hoping something sticks - is ineffective because there's no plan and an unrealistic expectation about the time needed to deliver results.
- Perfectionism marketing doesn't work because it's rarely implemented - there's always a need to re-write or proof it "just one more time."
- Ant marketing copies what your competitors are doing, but your competitors probably don't know any more than you do at this point. Even if they do, their strategy and approach may not work for your business.
- Once you've tried the other approaches, you throw your hands up and proclaim that it's hopeless... marketing doesn't work!

- While just over half of small businesses will outsource graphic design and website creation, only a fraction will outsource their marketing. It doesn't make any sense!
- Research has shown that entrepreneurs who handle their own marketing are the least satisfied with their results. They don't know what to do or they don't get it done.

EZ-er Way: Contact The Small Biz Marketing Specialist! *smallbizmarketingspecialist.com*

Chapter Two:

Compound Interest and Karate: Marketing Implications

"Compound interest is the eighth wonder of the world. He who understands it, earns it... he who doesn't, pays it."

That quote is often attributed to Albert Einstein, and no matter who actually said it, it's entirely true.

Consider this scenario: Two small business owners, Sam and John, start the exact same type of business on the exact same day. They both generate $2,000 a year that can be invested. Sam invests his $2,000 immediately and each year thereafter, from age 19 to age 26, invests another $2,000 annually… but not a penny more. At that time, John sees that Sam is doing pretty well and thinks he had better start saving for retirement also. He starts to invest $2,000 a year and continues funding it for 38 years (age 27 to 65).

At age 65, because of the beauty and power of compounding, Sam's retirement account is over $750,000 greater than John's. Sam invested $16,000, and the compounding interest created nearly $2.3 million by age 65. John, on the other hand, invested $76,000 and ended up with only $1.5 million. Because of compound interest, Sam was able to not only make over $750,000 more but cost $60K less to do so.

Age	Sam Invests:		John Invests:	
19	2,000	2,240	0	0
20	2,000	4,749	0	0
21	2,000	7,558	0	0
22	2,000	10,706	0	0
23	2,000	14,230	0	0
24	2,000	18,178	0	0
25	2,000	22,599	0	0
26	2,000	27,551	0	0
27	0	30,857	2,000	2,240
28	0	34,560	2,000	4,749
29	0	38,708	2,000	7,558
30	0	43,352	2,000	10,706
31	0	48,554	2,000	14,230
32	0	54,381	2,000	18,178
33	0	60,907	2,000	22,599
34	0	68,216	2,000	27,551
35	0	76,802	2,000	33,097
36	0	85,570	2,000	39,309
37	0	95,383	2,000	46,266
38	0	107,339	2,000	54,058
39	0	120,220	2,000	62,785
40	0	134,646	2,000	72,559
41	0	150,804	2,000	83,506
42	0	168,900	2,000	95,767
43	0	189,168	2,000	109,499
44	0	211,869	2,000	124,879
45	0	237,293	2,000	142,104
46	0	265,768	2,000	161,396
47	0	297,660	2,000	183,004
48	0	333,379	2,000	207,204
49	0	373,385	2,000	234,308
50	0	418,191	2,000	264,665
51	0	468,374	2,000	298,665
52	0	524,579	2,000	336,745
53	0	587,528	2,000	379,394
54	0	658,032	2,000	427,161
55	0	736,995	2,000	480,660
56	0	825,435	2,000	540,579
57	0	924,487	2,000	607,688
58	0	1,035,425	2,000	682,851
59	0	1,159,676	2,000	767,033
60	0	1,298,837	2,000	861,317
61	0	1,454,698	2,000	966,915
62	0	1,629,261	2,000	1,085,185
63	0	1,824,773	2,000	1,217,647
64	0	2,043,746	2,000	1,366,005
65	0	$2,288,996	2,000	$1,532,166

12% return

WOW!

While I've oversimplified the example just a bit, you get the picture. So here's my money advice: Start investing now and do it consistently. We'll see in a moment how the beauty of compounding can also leverage your small business marketing efforts.

"Long-term consistency trumps short-term intensity." ~ Bruce Lee

I've always loved the beauty of martial arts. The movements, the discipline, the confidence, the culture. Watching a skilled martial artist is like watching a professional dancer. The movements are smooth, controlled, and beautifully executed.

When my kids were growing up, together with my husband, they took karate lessons together. They all started at white belt. I would go to their classes many times and watch them do the same movement - whether a strike, a hold, a transition, or a series of movements - over and over and over again. Many times, only one single thing was repeated and reinforced during the class. Then they would come home and practice that same move over and over and

> Start with one thing and practice it repeatedly until you master it. Then move on.

over again until they were able to perform it with precision, grace, and strength time after time after time.

They were not allowed to move up in belts until everything from the previous belt was ***mastered***. There's a reason for that. The basics must be right - the hours of going to classes and practicing allowed them to ultimately attain their second-degree black belts. It didn't just "happen." It was achieved by mastering a skill and then adding on one more thing, and so on and so on.

Marketing Applications

Okay, so you should start investing now and practice repeatedly to master a karate move. What in the world does this have to do with marketing? A lot!

In order to grow your business, as with investing, you must be consistent in order to be successful. You need to consistently be marketing in order to see compounded results for your efforts - and a bigger bottom line, like Sam's. And also like the investment example I shared, the sooner you start, the better. That means doing something every day, every week, every month, every year! Unlike the investment example, however, you can't sit back and watch your business and profits continue to grow. You must keep at it, but as you do, you'll find it gets easier with less time and effort required. This is how you compound your efforts so that the results grow on their own over time. I assure you, your consistent marketing efforts will snow ball and take on their own momentum.

There's no denying that people who are successful in business rely on consistency. They are consistent in their marketing, their sales, the content they create, how often they post on social media, and even in their morning routines. So, if you want to get results from your marketing, logically, you need to be consistent.

> Consistent marketing will pay off in the form of more sales that lead to more profits and more money for you.

By results, I'm not talking about more followers, more reach, more awareness, or more leads. Sure, that stuff is important, but when I talk about results, I'm talking about converting more leads into prospects, more prospects into customers, and more customers into sales. More sales lead to more profits, and more profits lead to more money that you can invest to appreciate the beauty of compounding interest.

One of the most common reasons marketing campaigns in small businesses fail is because there's no consistency. There's no "compounding interest" and no momentum building.

A business owner hears the great success stories that others have had by gaining more followers on Twitter, generating more leads on Facebook, and increasing sales through content marketing. And what happens?

They think, "Oh wow, this sounds great! Let me try that."

They dabble in it for a bit, then stop.

Then they wonder, "Why didn't this marketing strategy work for me? Maybe it just doesn't work for my type of business...."

Well, when you dabble in your marketing, you're right! It won't work. If you invest a little and then stop, you'll never enjoy the benefits of compounding interest. Not because that marketing channel isn't suited to your business, but usually because you didn't maintain it long enough. Keep the investing example in mind: Sam didn't enjoy the beauty of compounding overnight. No one does. Part of that equation is time, and the same thing is true for marketing - it takes consistency and time.

The businesses that produce the best results (in terms of generating both leads ***and*** sales) are those that are consistent in their marketing. They've regularly been sending clear, consistent messages to potential clients. Not just for weeks or months, but for years.

I have a client who is a Realtor® in the greater Boston area. She came to me for marketing help three years ago because she wanted to become the #1 Realtor® in her area. She knew she needed to do marketing to make that happen, but she was stuck in "spaghetti marketing" to that point - doing a lot of "things" - always "busy" but nothing getting done and subsequently no results.

I put together a marketing plan for her that was very simple. Just a few things that we would wash, rinse, and repeat. A few things on which she could concentrate and practice, just like the repetition of a karate move to perfect it. The key component of the plan was content marketing - to position her as the "go-to" Realtor® because of her expertise of the area and because of her commitment to unparalleled service.

> As with mastering karate, to master marketing you must start with one thing and continue to hone that skill.

I didn't create lots of content for her and throw it up there, then move on to another marketing strategy. I started with ***one thing*** - and broke it into doable daily pieces that could be leveraged to achieve compounded growth.

The first step was keyword research - to find out what people were searching for and what type(s) of content we could create to answer their most pressing questions. Once that was done, I created one amazing piece of content - an eBook that was a lead generation piece. Then I repurposed that into a series of blog posts. Then I repurposed those into a series of social media posts. Then I repurposed it again into a series of videos.

The compounding of doing ***one thing*** well, then continuing to do it until it's perfected, then adding on more that grows on the basis of what's already been done, has allowed her to become the #1 Realtor® in her area. She shows up on the first page of Google for many real estate agent searches organically. Considering that those top slots are all big-name behemoths such as Zillow.com, Realtor.com, Trulia.com, and Redfin.com, that is truly phenomenal. She even beats out her brokerage in getting found online.

She's been able to build out a team who supports her real estate business, so she's only doing the parts of the process she loves. And now she has the time freedom she always wanted and is starting up a new venture to mentor both aspiring and/or struggling real estate agents to have a successful real estate business on their terms. She now has a business she loves, as well as the time freedom she wanted because she combined consistency and perfecting one or two things in order to enjoy the benefit of compound interest.

Yes, compound interest and karate really do have marketing implications!

Could you do ***one thing*** today to get your marketing kick started? Could you do one more thing tomorrow? And another thing the next day?

Yes, you can! You just need....

Get It Done the EZ Way:

- Compounding interest pays huge dividends when it comes to investments. It has a marketing application as well!
- To become a master, start with one thing and practice it repeatedly, then move on.
- You must consistently market to generate the results you want, and as you do, your marketing will gain momentum and get easier and easier.
- Create a simple marketing plan, then wash, rinse, and ***repeat***.
- Starting with one thing like an eBook opens the door to building that out to several other components that you can use for content marketing.

EZ-er Way: Contact The Small Biz Marketing Specialist! [*smallbizmarketingspecialist.com*](smallbizmarketingspecialist.com)

Chapter Three:

Get Your Marketing into ACTION!

Clients reach out to me to help get their marketing done because they've fallen into one of the marketing approaches mentioned previously: spaghetti marketing, perfectionism marketing, ant marketing, or hopeless marketing.

I can hear the frustration in their voices. They want to know what they can do to generate real business growth and profitability. They want a marketing plan they can create, follow, and then see results. But they're frustrated because they have no idea where to start. They've been wasting time and money with spaghetti, perfectionism, ant, or hopeless marketing. Do you find yourself in a similar situation? How much time and money have you been wasting?

Let me tell you what I tell them: Getting started is easy. You just need to take action – figuratively and literally. After I've explained how to take "action" and get started to my clients, they say, "Wow! You are the first person who explained it so simply. Yes, it completely makes sense. It's so easy!"

That's exactly why I wrote this book and titled it as I did: *Small Business Marketing Made EZ!*

Are you tired of being frustrated, wasting your time and money on marketing that is not generating the results you want and need? Are you ready to create the sales and marketing approaches that will help you bring in plenty of customers to grow - even explode - your business? Are you ready to make the most of the relationships you've built with your existing customers so that you can wow them and get referrals and repeat sales?

> When you take ACTION, you'll realize that your marketing can be easier and more effective than you ever imagined!

Of course you are!

I've developed ***the*** system to help you get out of survival mode and start to thrive, instead. It's the ACTION system:

- Attract
- Connect
- Transactions
- Invest
- Ongoing
- Nurture

ACTION Steps

ACTION can be applied to any business in any industry of any size to create marketing success and business growth. It will allow you to create a sustainable, repeatable, and profitable business. ACTION is a simple framework that will help you ATTRACT the right prospects, and CONNECT with them, so you can create profitable TRANSACTIONS. You'll make smart decisions, so you know where and how to INVEST in your marketing, which is not a "one and done." It's an ONGOING process in which you'll NURTURE the relationships you've created, so your customers, clients, or patients never imagine doing business with anyone else.

I guarantee it will help you see all of your revenue-generating activities more clearly and show you where you can focus to get the best results, really leveraging your efforts and boosting your ROI. The ACTION system is ***the*** solution to the biggest sales and marketing challenges that all small business owners face:

- Not attracting enough traffic to get real leads or prospects to whom you can sell.
- Not converting those leads and prospects into sales.
- Not investing your marketing time and dollars in the right places.

- Not leveraging your marketing efforts to stay front-of-mind with prospects, customers, and past customers.
- Not wowing your existing customers to generate easy and repeat business and get referrals.

Let's talk about each phase of the ACTION system.

> By following the ACTION system, you'll being attracting and connecting with the right customers, enjoying profitable transactions, investing in growth, and taking ongoing steps to really nurture relationships to explode your business!

ATTRACT helps you get clear about who your best customers, clients, or patients are - your target market - so you can create content, tools, and offers to attract interest, collect leads, and follow up without wasting a lot of time and money reaching the wrong audience who is probably never going to buy from you.

CONNECT helps you educate your target market and have conversations that build relationships with potential customers, so you're viewed as "the go-to solution." The goal is for your prospects to say, "This company gets me and understands the problems I'm facing!"

TRANSACTION helps you craft a strategy to make resonating offers to your best prospects and ensure you are not missing opportunities to encourage and inspire new customers to buy from you. When you make the right offer to the right person at the right time, price is rarely the consideration factor, thus maximizing your profit potential.

INVEST helps you understand where and how your customers are buying from you, so you can spend your valuable resources most effectively. You'll have the metrics you need to know what's working and what's not, so you can best leverage your efforts. It's not about doing "lots of things"; it's about "doing a few things well."

The **ONGOING** step helps you realize that marketing is not a "one and done." It's something that is a system, a process, that keeps you front-of-mind with your prospects and existing customers. It also maps out a sales process that gives people a reason to come back and buy from you again and again.

NURTURE helps you maximize the relationships you've built with the people who have already spent money with you. This always reminds me of a saying my dad jokes about having been married to my mom for over 50 years: "It's cheaper to keep'er." He's right. Repeat business is the best way to grow and boost your profitability. Existing customers are your best customers. You already know you'll spend far less money and effort selling to existing customers than trying to attract new ones. That's why it's important to wow your customers from the start with great value and a great experience.

With that overview of how to get your marketing into ACTION, let's delve deeper into why this system is so easy and how you can incorporate the ACTION marketing system in your business.

Get It Done the EZ Way:

- There is nothing as frustrating in business as wasting time and money on marketing that does not work.
- When you are ready to attract the right audience and make the most of the relationships you create to generate more repeat business and referrals, you'll be ready to take ACTION.
- The ACTION system will get you out of survival mode and enable your business to start thriving.
- Using the ACTION system, you'll be able to more clearly see what's working, so you can focus your efforts to leverage results and profitability.

EZ-er Way: Contact The Small Biz Marketing Specialist! smallbizmarketingspecialist.com

Chapter Four:

Attention

In order to effectively market your products and services, you must get the ATTENTION of your prospective customers, clients, or patients. Without drawing attention, nothing else really matters. Your business will be overlooked! You will not stand out from the crowd.

Here's what I've found most small business owners do to try to draw attention to themselves:

- Get really excited about all the different ways they can market their products and services.
- Throw up a website or sales page.
- Create offers, deals, and promotions.
- Design some cool graphics and images.
- Run some Facebook or Google ads.

Most small business owners have grand visions when they start their businesses. They want the whole world to know about who they are and what they do. Ask them who they serve, and they'll say ***anyone and everyone***. I call that "spray and pray."

If that's what you are doing… STOP! Stop it, right now!

Unless you're really, really lucky, I guarantee you are going to fail.

You know why? Because you need to consider whether your target market actually ***wants*** the damn thing you're offering, and if they do want it, what makes you think they'll buy it from ***you***?

> If you don't draw attention to your product or service and how it provides the solution, nothing else matters. But there's a right way to do it!

Now I'm not saying this to be rude or put a downer on your high. I'm saying it because it's a trap many business owners fall into. And trust me, I have fallen into this very trap myself.

When I started my coffee and smoothie business, I had no clear understanding of who my best customer was. I just wanted to sell a ton of coffees and smoothies – to anyone and everyone. What I learned the hard and expensive way is the advice I now teach my clients when it comes to getting attention: ***"You can't be everything to everyone. Instead be something for someone."***

Let me repeat that because it's critical: You cannot be everything to everyone. Be something for someone.

Get Specific

How do you become something for someone? You get crystal clear about ***who*** it is you serve and the ***unique*** solution you provide.

Here's how I converted from being everything to everyone to being something for someone in my coffee and smoothie business:

Instead of trying to sell coffees and smoothies to anyone who would buy them, I looked at where my biggest profitability came from and who was buying it - who was really generating that profit. My books clearly showed that the real money to be made was coming from catering, not selling coffees and smoothies one at a time. As I dug deeper into the data, I learned more about the person who was ordering those catering services. As I describe her, notice how specific I am in defining my best customer:

I figured out that my "someone" was Carol, the HR manager at a company with 50 to 100 employees who was struggling to find something fun, different, and healthy to offer employees for staff appreciation events. The types of events Carol was putting together were the typical pizza parties, ice cream socials, etc. Planning and organizing them took a lot of her time (time that she couldn't spend on her primary duties), and she rarely got any recognition for her efforts. The staff became bored of these typical events, so they rarely attended. By understanding the pain points, the goals, and a typical day for an HR manager, I was able to get her ATTENTION because I wasn't just "selling smoothies." I was helping her become the "Big Kahuna" in the office by taking staff to Hawaii with "The Ultimate Hawaiian Getaway Without a 12-Hour Flight." Staff could come up to an authentic Hawaiian tiki bar where professional "tikitenders" blended gourmet, all-natural fresh fruit smoothies topped off with a Hawaiian parasol. By letting Carol know she could treat her staff to a "vacation in a cup," Carol now feels I "get" her... I understand her frustration in putting fun staff appreciation events together. I speak her language. I offer solutions that make her job easy and make her look great. I've got her attention. I've become "something for someone."

As I was describing Carol, where she works, her challenges and pain in putting together staff appreciation events, did you get a clear picture in your head of "who" she is? That's exactly what you need to do. You need to be so crystal clear in who you're trying to get the attention of that you see that person just as if they're standing right in front of you. This will help tremendously when we get to the next step in the ACTION system.

The question you need to ask and answer is ***who*** is your ***best*** prospect?

> Be something for someone rather than trying to be everything to everyone!

Far too many business owners make the mistake of trying to appeal to too many people – to be everything to everyone. The key thing is you have to make a choice. Your product or service needs to appeal to one key persona, an avatar – a specific representation of the type of people who are hungry for or need what you're going to offer them. It needs to be so targeted and specific that it's as if you're having a one-on-one conversation with them where they say, "Yeah, you get me!"

Consider these examples of broad vs targeted avatars:

BROAD	TARGETED
Golfers	Left-handed, middle age male golfers who want to improve their short games.
Women	Females in their 20s who had a child in the last year and follow a vegan diet and are interested in health, wellness, and

	clean living on Facebook.
Homeowners	Homes that are 20+ years old owned by retiring baby boomers with incomes of $150,000-plus in Jacksonville, Florida interested in kitchen remodeling.
People who need to get their taxes done	Mid- to upper-income 30- to 60-year-olds who are motivated to save. They're married, with kids and a house. They feel good, even proud, doing things that save money—like do-it-yourself (DIY) projects. They file their own taxes because they believe it's relatively simple and saves accounting fees. But they're unaware that they're missing out on additional tax credits and deductions that could save them even more.

See the big difference? Being more targeted allows you to create a picture - literally - of that person. And truly that's what you want to do. You want to be so crystal clear in your ***who*** that you even have a name for that person, just like mine was "Carol, the HR manager."

I had one client who fell into the trap of "trying to be everything to everyone" and instead ended up being "no one to anyone." They thought their niche was dentists and that seemed targeted enough to them. However, in looking at the data, it became clear that not every dentist was the same. Some were just starting out and had much different goals than the dentist who was more established and looking to grow and open additional locations. Then there was the dentist who was looking to exit and retire yet have a sustainable retirement income. They were all in different places in their journeys through their careers, yet this client was sending out the same message to each one. No wonder they were frustrated that they weren't getting good results from their marketing.

> Without a very specific avatar, you cannot craft the marketing messages and tactics that will resonate.

I was able to help them define their key avatar - actually it ended up being six different avatars (reflecting some of the specific differences I just mentioned) - and by doing so, we could then better understand each group's needs, challenges, and opportunities, so we could create specific messages that would resonate with each group. Their marketing results immediately improved because they were now "being something for someone."

Getting attention is about segmenting and creating niches as small and specific as possible, so you can easily get the attention of that group. By understanding their needs, challenges, pain points, and opportunities, you'll be much better positioned to "speak their language" and be viewed as the solution since you "get them."

Here are some questions you can ask yourself to figure out who your customer avatar is:

1. Who is your ideal customer? Describe them in as much detail as you possibly can. What is their age, occupation, gender? What hobbies do they have? What is their name?
2. How do they consume their information? What magazines do they read? What do they watch on TV? What social media platforms do they hang out on?

3. What are their goals and values? Think about this question in relation to your product or service. What is important to them that by using your product or service will help them achieve their goals or relieve their pain?
4. What emotions do they have? This is similar to goals and values, but goes deeper, to the core of their problem or issue. How do they ***feel*** before and after using your product or service?
5. What are their fears and pain points? Are they afraid of losing money? Losing business? Do they lack in confidence or knowledge?
6. Who is their nemesis? Is the enemy the bank manager who wouldn't lend them money? The people who never believed in them? The noisy neighbors who keep them up at night?
7. What gets them excited? What makes them so happy they're grinning from ear to ear? What does success mean to them?
8. What's a typical day in the life of your customer avatar? What are the frustrations they encounter? What prevents them from meeting their goals?

Once you've answered these questions, you've already built up a clearer picture of who your product or service needs to appeal to… because you've gotten very, very specific. You have now defined how you offer something for someone.

I've included a template for this exercise in the Resources section at the end of the book for handy reference. Simply fill in each area to get crystal clear about ***who*** it is you serve. I encourage my clients to keep this in front of them every day, so they're reminded of exactly who their best customers are – that they're something for someone.

Are They Qualified?

Now that you've determined your "who," you need to make sure they're actually qualified, or they may not be worth your marketing efforts. Here's why: Let's say you sell personal training services. You've defined your perfect avatar – the middle-aged, mid- to senior-level executive who is 25 pounds overweight, travels a bit for work, and therefore, doesn't eat the healthiest and never seems to find the time to work out.

> A specific avatar isn't enough. You must have qualified prospects in order to make the most of your marketing efforts.

Does that mean that every person who fits this description that you attract and get attention from will be a qualified prospect?

In a word, no.

You could waste a lot of time and money marketing to an unqualified prospect, even if they do fit into your avatar or niche. We have to drill down a bit deeper to discover your qualified target prospect. So how do you define a qualified prospect?

I use the acronym PAIN because it's a word that has literal and figurative meaning:

P, Problem: A qualified avatar must have a problem that your product, service, or solution can solve; otherwise, they're probably not a good fit. If they do have the problem you can successfully address, then they need to move to the next step.

A, Acknowledge: A qualified avatar must acknowledge the fact that they have a problem. If the person doesn't acknowledge it, it's as if the problem doesn't exist. Yes, they're only kidding themselves, but in doing so, they won't pay attention to your solution. When someone acknowledges a problem, they'll be willing to look for a solution. They'll be willing to have a conversation with you about how you can solve their problem.

I, Inspired: Your best prospect must be inspired to find a solution. Not only does your prospect have to have a problem and acknowledge they have a problem, they must be inspired to find the solution. They have to get off of their rear end and do something about it. They have to take action.

N, Necessary Authority: A qualified avatar must have the necessary authority to implement your solution. By necessary authority, I mean they must have the budget or be empowered to make a buying decision. They must be able to work with you for you to consider them a qualified prospect

PAIN is actually a good thing for you as a small business owner. You want your prospect to have it (problem, acknowledgment, inspiration, and necessary authority) because it's your product, service, or solution that will alleviate the pain. In the next chapter, I'll show you how to find these qualified prospects and what to say to them when you do.

> When your prospect has "PAIN," you are on your way to having a qualified prospect. Get ***their*** attention!

When you are crystal clear on your ***who*** - who it is you serve and provide solutions for, you'll find that you're not only getting the attention of the perfect customer, client, or patient who is your avatar and best audience, but you'll make a lot more money with a lot less effort.

What you'll find is: ***"There are riches in niches."***

When you're very, very specific in who you serve, and create your marketing efforts to be targeted to that niche, you'll find it's like building a fence around that group. They will be so committed to you that they won't even think of going anywhere else. You are now the "go-to" person. Price will not be their determining factor. Your ability to provide solutions that specifically address their needs, concerns, and pain points is all that will matter.

Your goal is to actually get fewer eyes but more focused buyers. That may seem counterintuitive, but you will never be profitable if you continue trying to be everything to everyone. The ability to grow your business and increase your profitability lies in your ability to be something for someone. The power - and the profit - is in getting attention from your qualified audience. Once you narrow this down, you will discover real marketing power! People will start coming to you. You'll hear them say, "Oh my gosh, it's like you were talking directly to me."

When you hear that, you'll know you've struck gold. ***That's the power behind very specifically defining your target market to get the right attention.***

Get It Done the EZ Way:

- If you don't first draw attention to the solution you offer through your product or service, nothing else matters. This is the critical first step.

- Trying to be everything to everyone? Stop it, right now. Instead you must be something for someone.
- You must get laser-beam specific about who your target audience really is in order for your marketing to be effective.
- The more specifically you can define your avatar, the better off you'll be... including giving this person a name!
- Your avatar should think, "Yeah, they really get me!"
- Be sure to use the template I've created for you to hone in on who your best customer, client, or patient really is.
- Once you define your avatar, you must also qualify them. Even if a prospect meets your definition, they may not be qualified to buy from you.
- Use PAIN (problem, acknowledgment, inspiration, and necessary authority) to qualify your prospects.
- There are riches in niches!

EZ-er Way: Contact The Small Biz Marketing Specialist! smallbizmarketingspecialist.com

Chapter Five:

Connect

Now that you know ***who*** your best customers, clients, or patients are, you're ready to CONNECT with them. You connect with what you say and where you say it, so let's jump into that in this chapter.

When you get the attention of prospective new customers, clients or patients, it's easy to "get into sales mode" and start shoving stuff down their throats with "Buy! Buy! Buy!" messages. After all, someone might be interested right now and you just want to make sales and close some business, right?

STOP!

If you had just gotten the attention of the most gorgeous/handsome gal/guy and you want to ask them on a date, would your first question be, "Will you marry me?"

No! Of course not! That would be really creepy and disconcerting to the person you're asking, and you'll no doubt find you have a very low response rate to say nothing of making no progress toward the altar or, in our case, the sale. You're not connecting… you're disconnecting. Even worse than disconnecting, you're alienating because this person now never wants to see or hear from you again.

However, this is exactly what small business owners do. They get so excited that they've gotten someone's attention, they want to immediately ask for marriage - the sale.

Connecting is about building a relationship, being a go-giver, and doing all the right things so that the gal/guy (aka your prospect) does want to see and hear from you again - and again - and again - so much so, they actually look forward to seeing and hearing from you. In the dating example, your goal is to get from that first meeting to a next date - perhaps a cup of coffee, to then another date - perhaps dinner and movie, up until it's clear this is a perfect match and is meant to be. At that point when you ask, "Will you marry me?" you can be pretty sure the answer is going to be yes.

From the first thing you say or do to get the attention of your prospective spouse to the day you get married (and quite honestly every day thereafter - take it from someone who's been married over 27 years), connecting is about doing something to move a relationship positively forward day by day. It's about providing value (and fun little surprises) that the other side is excited to receive and makes them want

> Take time to connect. You shouldn't propose marriage on the first date!

more and more from you. They want to remain connected to you!

It's about Them!

So what ***do*** you say to that "hunk a hunk a burning love" you see on the opposite side of the room who could be your next customer, client, or patient? How can you get their attention?

You craft a ***message*** that resonates with ***them***, that speaks their language, and gets them interested in learning more. It's not at all about what you might want to say; it's about what they want to hear. Position yourself as different and help them to understand that you are not a commodity - you're not the "same old, same old."

Here is where most small business owners get it wrong. They want to beat their chests because they're so proud of what they do. The messaging is all "I, I, I" and "We, We, We." Take a look at your "About Us" page on your website. How many "I's" and "We's" do you find? Read the emails you send out. Look at the posts you put on social media. You'll quickly see what I mean. And guess what? Your prospect doesn't care about you. The only thing they care about is WIIFM - What's In It For Me?!?

I have an accounting firm as a client, and they wanted to work with small business owners but weren't having any success getting traction in the marketplace. They couldn't get the attention of the small business owners that were their target market. I asked them, "What makes you great?" You could hear the excitement over the phone as they spilled out their reply. It was as if I could see them pounding their chests while they told me, "We have great results. Our staff has years of experience. We do high quality work. We've been in business 35 years."

Notice the words they used? "We… We… We."

I carefully said, "Yes, I can tell you're proud of what you feel makes ***you*** great. But that's exactly what your competitors all say, too. You're not going to connect and get that prospect interested in what you do simply by bragging about yourself."

After better understanding what this accounting firm provided and how they did it, I rebranded them as "The Small Biz Profit Defender." That's language that resonates with a small business owner. Instead of working with an "accounting firm," they're working with a "small business profit ***defender***" – a firm that is going to help them budget, save money on taxes, and defend the profits they make.

> Watch for "We," "Us," and "I" in your marketing messages. It's not about you.

See the big difference?

I did the same thing in my own coffee and smoothie business. Sure, I sell coffees and smoothies. Talk about a commodity! I also sell catering services. Talk about competitive... especially in the Washington, D.C. area! Imagine competing against that where there are two Starbucks on every street in a non-small-business-friendly city with heavy competition for corporate catering.

There was no way I was going to get any business by saying I offered "coffee and smoothie catering services." Snore, bore, no one cares!

What I did instead was offer "The Ultimate Hawaiian Getaway Without a 12-Hour Flight" where an HR or office manager can be "The Big Kahuna." As I shared earlier, guests would come up to an authentic tiki bar where professional "tikitenders" blend gourmet all-natural fresh fruit smoothies topped off with a Hawaiian parasol. No wonder people call us a "vacation in a cup!"

Now which would you prefer:

- A smoothie ***or*** a "vacation in a cup"
- Catering ***or*** The Ultimate Hawaiian Getaway Without a 12-Hour Flight
- Catering staff ***or*** "tikitenders"

The language I use creates a vision of what they're going to get. I'm able to connect with my target audience (HR and/or office managers) because they want to do something fun and different for staff to keep morale high, recognize staff, and show appreciation. It's not their full-time job to handle the catering, and, as I mentioned, they never get any appreciation or recognition for the events they do plan. These HR/office managers would love to be called "The Big Kahuna" because everyone had such a great time and loved the smoothies and lavished praise on them afterwards. If I were to say, "Hey we'll come in and serve smoothies for one of your events," do you think my calendar would be full with catering jobs? Of course not. There's no connection.

I am able to connect and use messaging that resonates with the specific audience I'm addressing. Messaging can be words. Messaging can be images. Ultimately, it makes your target audience take notice and say, "Yes, that's me! I want to learn more."

In building that connection and creating your messages, it's important to understand that people buy on emotion more often that they like to admit. Yes, many people shop price, quality, and value; however, even rational decisions are unknowingly influenced by the right side of the brain - the creative, emotional side. When rational thinking doesn't quite add up, the emotional synapses kick into high gear and take over the process. The vision of a Hawaiian getaway is far more emotionally appealing than simply envisioning a fruit smoothie, no matter how nice that smoothie may look. With a well-crafted message, you can have emotion trump logic almost every time!

Crafting an Emotional Message

Here are five tips to help you build more emotion into your messages, so you more effectively connect with your prospects.

1) **Speak to your target customer, client, or patient directly.** Don't speak to the masses. Yes, you want to appeal to many, but speak to one - your customer avatar. You now know who that is since you perfected it in the last chapter. I'm sure you have wonderful customers, clients, or patients with whom you interact. They provide valuable feedback regarding your company's products and services. Think about them as you're crafting your messaging. Speak ***directly*** to them. Talk to them like you're sitting across the dinner table from one another. This "voice" is what you'll use in your content and social media communications. One-on-one communication is much more intimate and engaging than a mega-horn. It's certainly more emotional.
2) **Create unique, valuable insights that can only come from you, not your competitors.** People love exclusivity. Give your audience something they can't find anywhere else, and they'll automatically gravitate toward you and spread the word about your

products and services. This is especially true if you're giving these insights away for free. Show your audience that you have something valuable to offer, and you'll see your audience come back again and again.

3) **Use humor, compassion, and empathy.** Never underestimate the power of emotions. If someone can make you smile or shed a tear, you know there's a pretty strong emotional bond. These emotions are great to tap into because as humans, ***we love to relate***. Make an inside joke that only your audience will understand, go for it! Or if you've recently experienced an issue that your audience can relate to, tell them about it and explain how you resolved it. Your audience needs to see that ***your company is built with real people*** - that it has a face and a personality that people can relate to and engage with.
4) **Pick a side and make your case.** Going back to #2 on this list, ***your audience looks to you as the expert*** to solve their problems. In order to be considered an expert, not only must you provide valuable insights, but you must also take a firm stance. Back up your points with hard evidence. ***Maintain your credibility by accurately citing your sources and imagery.*** Be

objective and professional. Think about political candidates running for office. They're ineffective when they're not 100 percent for or against a particular policy. They appear indecisive, weak, and untrustworthy. That's why you need to remain very clear-cut. No one likes a flip-flopper.

5) **Ask the right questions to make them think.** The easiest way to connect emotionally and drive more engagement among your audience is to question them. Ask them about their experiences with your company, your products, or your service. Is there a hot topic about which you know your audience wants to hear your opinion? Give it to them with your solid stance, and then ask them if they agree and why or why not. ***Encourage healthy debate.***

Why and Where

In crafting your message that gets to the "emotion" and allows you to more effectively connect with your audience, instead of saying what you do, say ***why you do it***. That answers why your prospects should care and what's in it for them. Answer how this particular product or service fits into their lives and benefits them. The "why" in the answer is the reason most people will buy from you.

Once you nail down the "why" for your company into a compelling elevator speech, marketing messages in all other forms fall into place.

Now that you know how to connect with your audience and the messaging you can use that will resonate with them to get attention and interest, you need to know ***where*** to place those messages so that they're seen. You will have to uncover the right media.

> Nail down the answer to "why" for your company, and the rest of your marketing messages will fall into place.

Today there's no shortage of media choices. There's online media such as social media, websites, PPC, email, content (various formats), SEO, and mobile marketing. There's offline media such as direct mail, TV, radio, magazines, newspapers, and billboards. And of course, there are a myriad of miscellaneous areas that can be considered as well. For example, closed-circuit TV at health clubs, word of mouth, events and seminars, bus wraps, power point presentations, demonstrations, etc.

I could write an entire book just on all of the different media available, the pros and cons of each, and how to use them in your small business marketing plan. The question most small business owners ask is, "How do I choose?" But that's not the right question to ask!

If you've followed the steps so far, picking the right media is easy because you know your audience and you know where they "hang out."

In my coffee and smoothie business, I know that three media work extremely well:

- LinkedIn: My audience hangs out on LinkedIn (because as an HR manager, they're always looking for new talent), so creating valuable content and messaging targeted to that audience works well.
- Associations: I also know that my audience belongs to the Society of Human Resource Managers (SHRM), so I'm a member and participate in and sponsor events on a local level.
- Direct Mail: I've created a "smoothie in a box" package that I send to my target audience. It's lumpy, interesting mail that is a "shock and awe" package that works extremely well because it stands out from the clutter and gets opened.

These are not the "cheapest" media, but they provide a huge ROI (return on investment) because I am connecting directly with my perfect avatar. It's where they hang out and where I can most effectively connect with them. While the competition is stupidly throwing dollars at other media where they're all competing against each other (e.g., Google AdWords), I'm directly connecting with my audience and finding minimal competition. I've created a market-message-media match, and my bottom line thanks me for it.

When you've chosen your target market correctly, use messaging that resonates with them, and put those messages in media where that target market "hangs out," you'll find that you quickly become the "go-to" expert. You'll be able to charge handsomely for your products and services and get paid for it by customers, clients, or patients who love you for the solutions you provide.

One final note on picking the right media: Remember that your target market hangs out in different places online and offline. An integrated marketing approach will bring you better results than relying solely on one medium. People respond to each type of media differently, remember them differently, and engage with them differently.

When you use an integrated marketing approach, all your tactics work together as a unified force, rather than allowing each to work in isolation. This maximizes efficiency and cost effectiveness to break through the clutter and connect with your target audience... making your marketing EZ and boosting your bottom line!

Get It Done the EZ Way:

- Your first contact with prospects cannot be a "Buy! Buy! Buy!" message. You have to connect with them before they will pay attention.
- As with developing a personal relationship, your first question when meeting someone can't be a proposal for marriage. That is not only disconnecting, it's downright alienating.
- You have to build a relationship, be a go-giver, and do the right things in order to make your prospect want to hear from you again and remain connected to you.
- Your message cannot focus on what you want to say. It must be about what the prospect wants to hear!
- Employ the five tips I shared in order to instill emotion into your message. Emotional messages are more powerful.
- Don't say what you do; say ***why*** you do it. The "why" is the reason people buy.
- Make certain you are sharing your message on the right platform and using the right media.

EZ-er Way: Contact The Small Biz Marketing Specialist! *smallbizmarketingspecialist.com*

Chapter Six:

Transaction

Now that you know ***who*** your perfect customer is, ***what*** to say to them, and ***where*** to put your message, then and only then are you ready for this next step.

I know what you're thinking. I can see the dollar signs in your eyes and the coins drooling from your mouth. You are ready for it... so ready for it... ready to make a sale!

A transaction. Lots of them.

Again. STOP!

Sorry, the sale and the ring of the cash register (or notification from PayPal) is not what I mean by transaction. At least not yet. It is really important that you fully understand the type of transaction I'm talking about as part of the ACTION system because this stage is where most small business owners fail. I don't want you to be in that category.

As "Small Business Stacey," I'm all about supporting small and local businesses. A new deli recently opened down the street from me. I was so excited to get a New York-style Reuben sandwich, but I left quite disappointed. My disappointment was not because of the food. In fact, my sandwich was actually delicious. I left the deli feeling so disappointed because this small business treated me like a transaction – simply as a sale and a ring on their cash register. They did nothing to get my contact information; they didn't invite me to join their loyalty program (they didn't even have one); they didn't ask where or how I heard about them; they didn't ask me to leave a review despite my telling the waitress this was the "best sandwich ever and had my taste buds begging for more!" This deli treated me like a simple transaction, not a customer with whom they wanted to create a relationship. I left and so did my money. I haven't been back since. Sure it was a great sandwich, but it's not my job as the customer to remember to do business with you. If that business had done just a few simple things to treat me as a person rather than as a transaction, I would be a regular – easily eating there once a week. Of course, I'd also rave to my friends, post about it on social media, and bring friends and family there as well, thus increasing the business this deli would get. Because this business treated me as a transaction, they got a one-time sale of $10. Had they followed my ACTION system, this business would have easily made a minimum of $10/week… $520/year. That's just for me and my one sandwich. It doesn't factor in

> Redefine "transaction." It's so much more than the ring of your cash register.

me bringing my husband with me, ordering additional items, referring my friends and family… and possibly most importantly, boasting about the deli on social media. That is easily worth another $520/year, and I'm being very conservative in my estimate. So this business lost over $1,000/year from just one customer. Multiply that by 100 and you can see the significant impact that makes. Here's the irony: This same business will be whining in a few months that "they have no customers" and "marketing doesn't work."

Unfortunately, that's how most small business owners treat their customers, clients or patients: as a transaction - literally… in the door, out the door… in the door, out the door. The problem is that there are many doors - online and offline - and everyone who interacts with your business is in a different place in their customer journey with you. Some may have stopped in your physical location. Some may have found you online. Some may have never heard of you before. Some may have heard of you but have never done business with you. Some may be actively seeking what you offer. Some may be considering options for what you offer. Some may not even realize that there's a solution for their problem and that you offer it. Some may have requested information to learn more about your products or services. Some may have already purchased from you. Some may have purchased but then never repurchased. There are obviously many touchpoints along the customer journey.

Touchpoints

Each of these touchpoints represents a transaction. Each is a "sale" - not necessarily monetarily but a sale in that it's the starting point to get to the next step in the relationship, whatever that may be. It is so important that you understand that a transaction is not a single event. It's not a "one and done."

The first transaction is the beginning of your relationship. It's what you do and how you treat people so they have an amazing experience that connects and guides them toward a positive next step or transaction.

I work with a client who sells vitamin supplements online. As we started working together, it became clear that they were treating everyone as a transaction. They only cared about the monetary sale, nothing else. If someone bought something, great. But that was it. No follow-up. No marketing to build multiple transactions. If someone filled their virtual shopping cart with products but then left, this client did nothing to follow up with that abandoned cart.

Everyone was treated the same, regardless of whether they were just looking for information about supplements to the person who had ordered multiple times and was obviously comfortable and happy with the product. The messaging was the same; the marketing was the same – all focused on "Buy! Buy! Buy! Let me shove some more supplements down your throat"… literally.

The majority of the people visiting their site did not buy. I knew this from reviewing their analytics. There was nothing in place to educate, to capture leads, to build a list. They didn't realize that they were leaving money on the table – literally – by treating everyone only as a monetary transaction. They thought if they just focused on doing more "email" or "social media" or "content marketing," they'd get more sales.

> Continue to build positive touchpoints for your customer in their journey through your sales funnel.

I was able to help them get a marketing plan in place that builds multiple positive transactions – touchpoints – across the customer journey, whether it's someone just visiting the site for the first time or a regular repeat customer. It meets the person where they are in the journey and where they want to go. It is 180-degrees different from what my client was doing before. Instead of focusing inward on, "How can we make more sales?," they now have a marketing plan that focuses on what really matters:

"How can we provide value, and excite and delight those who come into our world?"

They're still doing email, social media, and content marketing (actually my company does it for them). We've helped them increase sales by 42 percent by implementing the ACTION system and creating a process to ensure every interaction with a lead, prospect, customer, or past customer is a positive transaction.

If you've been following the ACTION system so far, you've already got their attention. You've made a connection. It is in this stage of the ACTION system in which you will make or break the possibility of a next step. Small business owners get it wrong in this stage when they think it's about them… making a sale. It's not. It's about focusing on what really matters to the prospect based on where they are in the relationship with you. Consumers will only pay attention to you when they're motivated to do so, and the best way to gain their attention is through interaction and education.

It's about meeting that person where they are now and helping them based on where they are ***in the relationship with you***. That next step will be different for everyone. That's why it's important to remember that in business people do business with people, and they'll buy when they're ready - not when you're ready.

Get Personal!

How can you ensure that every transaction you have is a step that moves that relationship forward? Simple: Get personal and personalize your communications.

Ever get those "Dear Neighbor" letters? How does it make you feel? I immediately throw mine in the circular file. It's obvious they know nothing about me - nor took the time to find out - so to me, they don't care. If you aren't willing to take the time to know anything about me, why should I take the time to know anything about you? Whoever is doing their marketing needs to read this book and contact me immediately!

Or have you received an email that, although it's been personalized with your name "Dear Sue," it has content that is of no interest to you and was obviously sent to everyone? That's like intruding into Sue's kitchen and dumping a pile of meats on her counter when she's a vegetarian. She's not going to be interested in it at all, and the fact that you intruded her personal space (aka her inbox) and wasted her time will only annoy her and leave a negative impression. "But email is free" is ***not*** a valid reason or even an excuse. It's just lazy marketing.

Personalization isn't about a simple greeting. It's about understanding the behavior and interests of your customers, then tailoring your messaging around that behavior and those interests.

I regularly buy my beauty products at a popular store. Every month for the past several years, this store has been sending out colorful flyers with monthly or seasonal discounts to me. I stopped reading the flyers because they were always the same and seemed impersonal. It was apparent that everyone was getting the same flyer at the same time, and what was being promoted was rarely for products that interested me - or that I've even purchased in the past. I never felt that the flyers had anything to do with me, other than the fact that I was a customer with a track record of shopping at this store. And here's the rub: Although I had made purchases on a number of occasions, I didn't feel loyal to the store.

> Personalizing your marketing message goes much deeper than the salutation line!

Then something interesting happened. I started getting a different kind of flyer. This time, it was personalized to me. It not only included my name, it said that a product that I had bought two months ago was now on sale. And because I liked that product, they suggested I try a new, related product that complemented my original purchase. If I bought both together, I'd receive a bundled deal plus a bonus. It wasn't a big deal, but now I felt that they were addressing ***me*** and that they had taken the time to suggest something personal that fit my situation. They weren't simply sending a generic flyer meant for their entire customer base.

Creating personalized communications doesn't have to take a lot of time nor cost a lot of money. Simple things like sending a birthday card or a handwritten note are easy ways to build and reinforce a positive connection.

You can also personalize your communications with touchpoints. You could follow up with a personalized call a day after you've done plumbing work in someone's home to ensure the work was satisfactory. Or tweeting key prospects personally with a relevant link related to something in which they'd be interested. Or sending an email invitation to a webinar to learn more about the topic for which they just requested your free ebook.

These are each transactions - "mini sales" that move the relationship forward. These are little things that keep your business front-of-mind and go a long way in building that "know, like, trust" factor that ultimately does lead to the transaction you want - a sale.

Be Relevant

In order to keep building your relationship transaction by transaction, you must also offer relevant content.

If your content is irrelevant to the reader, it is simply bad content. For example, if I'm thinking of changing the landscaping in my backyard and I'm researching what's involved, I'm going to be turned off if the only content I'm getting is "Buy this tree; buy this plant; buy this shrub." I'm not yet ready to buy.

It's important to understand your target customer and where they are in their consumer journey with you before you can create content that's relevant to them. Are you speaking to a prospect, a lead, a customer, or past customer? Make sure the content addresses their needs and that it is something the reader would want to consume.

What questions are your customers asking? Every day, your potential customers go online in search of information and answers. Knowing what those questions are gives you an unparalleled advantage in presenting targeted solutions with your content. It's also important to know what stage of the customer journey the targeted reader is in. Does the content give them next steps and progress them further through the sales funnel? Create each piece of content with the intent to trigger specific actions in your readers.

The best way to make a connection with people through your content is to speak as if you were across the dining room table. As I've said, one-on-one communication is more engaging. Write in the same language they use and be consistent with it. Write in the right tone and with the right attitude that appeals to the people for whom you're writing. Avoid jargon or language they don't understand. If you have to use technical terms, make sure to explain them clearly. For example, if your target audience is teen guys who are into cars and use slang, then communicate like them. You wouldn't want to sound formal and corporate-speak.

> Be relevant or your prospect won't read... let alone care about what you have to say.

When it comes to offering relevant content, it's also important to think about how you're presenting it, especially when it comes to web content. Use page elements wisely and tailor the design of your content for your users. Use the right font size, the right font style, color, etc. Use images that will resonate with your audience.

The best way to know if your content is relevant is to put yourself in your audience's shoes and answer these questions:

- Does this content fit my readers' needs?
- Am I talking to them directly?
- Will they like this?
- Will this help solve their problems?
- Will they learn something from this?
- Will they want to know more?

Remember people do business with those they know, like and trust. When you're consistently providing content that is helpful and being a go-giver without the pressure of "selling," then and only then do you have the right to ask for the sale.

Moving the transaction forward and asking for the sale boils down to asking these two questions:

1. Have I been truly generous to this individual and earned enough trust that they're ready to listen to my "ask"?
2. Do I 100 percent believe in the value of the solution I'm offering?

If the answer to these two questions is yes, you'll often find a transaction further deepens your relationship with your customer.

I love this quote from Dan Kennedy that sums this all up: "You don't get a customer to make a sale. You make a sale to get and keep a customer." Rather than look at customers, clients, or patients as a single transaction, treat them as a long-term, lifelong relationship. It completely changes how you approach your marketing.

Creating effective transactions really all comes down to putting yourself in your customer's shoes when you plan your customer journey. ***Allow the customer to define the terms of their relationship with you.*** When you do these things you're building on those transactions, and those you interact with will feel a loyalty toward your business and return for future purchases.

Buying Readiness

If you've followed my ACTION system thus far, you have the attention of your perfect customer, you've connected with them, and you've got them to raise their hand saying "***Yes!*** I want to know more."

That's doesn't mean that they're necessarily ready to buy at this point. It does mean they're ready to enter into a transaction with you, meaning they're ready to listen, to learn more, and to find out why you may be the answer to their prayers for their pains, struggles, and challenges.

Everyone is not going to be ready to buy at this point, but "No" doesn't mean no. No just means "Not right now." So you need to keep building transactions that strengthen the relationship and keep you front-of-mind. You want to make sure they don't leave and forget about you.

Someone who does this brilliantly is my friend, mentor and coach, Jim Palmer. I came into Jim's world years ago. I started watching his videos and listening to his podcasts. For years, I never purchased anything. But Jim showed up regularly and consistently in my inbox providing valuable and actionable information that was helping my business grow. Each interaction was a transaction. Jim started offering his Dream Business Academy, a live program where he teaches small business owners how to build their dream businesses. At this point in my life, I had dabbled with the idea that I wanted to provide done-for-you marketing services to small business owners, but it wasn't really going anywhere. Since the Dream Business Academy was coming to my area, I registered - a monetary transaction. I think it was about $200 to attend the two-day event. It was a low-cost way for me to dip my toes in the water and get some insight on creating my dream business.

It was a fantastic event, and I was given the opportunity to join Jim's coaching and mastermind program. Because of personal things happening at the time such as fighting off a bank that was threatening to take my home (the topic of my next book perhaps… lol), putting two kids through college, and my husband who was having health issues for which no one could tell him what was wrong, I said no to joining Jim's program.

Most small business owners would have stopped there. They would have taken the $200 sale, moved on, and started over again looking for new leads. But Jim is not like most small business owners, and I don't want you to be like most small business owners either.

What Jim did was to realize that "No" didn't mean no. No meant "Not right now." He continued to stay in touch, continued to provide valuable information and resources. He didn't pressure me to do something I wasn't ready for nor would be comfortable with. He let me stay in the stage of the customer journey I was in, and he just kept showing up day after day - via my inbox, via social media, via direct mail - with valuable and helpful resources. He was front-of-mind, so when I was ready to move to the next stage - aka another transaction - he would be the first person I thought of.

> Interpret "No" as "Not right now" and be politely persistent.

My situation improved. The threat of the bank taking my home was positively resolved. There was enough money in the bank to get my kids through college. My husband went gluten-free and miraculously his health problems went away. I was in a completely different place in my life ready to focus on building my dream business without any distractions.

Who do you think I was going to look to for help in doing that? Google? Someone who sent me a generic email promising me they can fix everything with their magic wand?

I already knew who I wanted to work with. Jim. The guy who stayed front-of-mind. The guy who helped me by being a go-giver without pressuring me to buy. The guy who realized that "No" didn't mean no. No meant "Not now." And because of that, I am now a VIP coaching client paying a handsome fee to be a part of his program.

Everything Jim did to move me forward in my customer journey was a transaction, a "mini sale." It may not have necessarily had a monetary value to it, but it moved the relationship forward, ultimately leading to a monetary transaction. Instead of Jim making a one-time $200 sale, he built a transaction - aka relationship - worth more than 20 times that.

Which type of transaction would you rather have in your business?

Embrace this stage of the ACTION system and create transactions that move the relationship forward.

To do that you need to provide ***value***.

Content is a great way to do that.

There's Value in Content

When it comes to creating content, it can seem overwhelming. There are so many different types - blog posts, infographics, social media posts, video. You're reading this book because you want something easy that you can get done fast and for which you can start seeing results. Many small business owners come to me for help in creating and managing their whole content marketing strategy, but you can do it yourself.

I advise my clients to focus on only one type of content to start: a lead magnet.

What is a lead magnet?

A lead magnet is anything of value that you can exchange for a prospect's contact information - at a minimum an email address. Their contact information is the currency they'll use for your lead magnet.

The most common types of lead magnets are tip sheets, free reports, white papers, ebooks, cheat sheets, or free trials. Lead magnets can also be videos, courses, quizzes, assessments, or challenges. Your lead magnet has one goal: to maximize the number of targeted leads you are getting for an offer.

A lead magnet is ***not*** these five words:

"Subscribe to my email newsletter"

No one wants to subscribe to your email newsletter. What they want is a solution to their problem.

It doesn't matter what type of lead magnet format you choose. The purpose of it is to ***educate*** not ***sell***. It needs to answer the questions they have and address the things they care about. The sale will come when the buyer is ready to buy which happens after you've had a number of positive transactions with them.

What a lead magnet doesn't need to be is lengthy of complex. Or time-intensive to create. In fact, a long and complex lead magnet will most likely convert poorly.

The only purpose of your lead magnet is to solve a ***specific problem*** with a ***specific solution*** for a ***specific segment*** of your audience.

Here are some questions to help you determine what type of lead magnet to create:

- What questions do potential customers typically have before they buy from me (product details, cost, warranty, social proof, etc.)?
- What does your market ***really*** want?
- How can I best address those concerns (tip sheet, white paper, videos)?

You've now learned that this stage of the ACTION system is about transactions that move the relationship forward. Most small business owners do it completely backward. They start by focusing on making a sale (to anyone), so they throw an ad out there, see who responds to it, then call that respondent their customer. It's completely backward and a huge waste of money!

When you are so crystal clear on who your target market is and you know what to say to them and where to say it, you actually won't have to "make a sale," the sales will come to you!

Get It Done the EZ Way:

- Focusing on transactions that represent a cash register ring or notification from PayPal will never get you more of those.
- If you treat your customers, clients, or patients as nothing more than a sale, you will never grow your business and will struggle to be profitable.
- Prospects may interact with you through various touchpoints, and each prospect will be at a different place in their journey through your sales funnel.
- Get personal with your audience and that goes far beyond simply knowing their name. You must also be aware of their interests.
- Provide content and information that is ***relevant*** to your prospects, customers, clients, or patients. Doing so builds the "know, like, and trust" factor.
- Getting a "No" doesn't necessarily mean no. It usually means "Not right now."

- There's value in content, so develop the lead magnet that is right for your business.

EZ-er Way: Contact The Small Biz Marketing Specialist! smallbizmarketingspecialist.com

Chapter Seven:

Invest

At this point, if you've been putting my ACTION system into action (and why wouldn't you because it is so EZ!), you're at the point at which you have money flowing into your business. Things are looking great. You've defined your perfect customer, client, or patient; you know where they hang out; you know what messaging resonates with them; you're providing valuable and helpful content; and not only are people starting to know, like and trust you - they're doing business with you. Congrats!

You now have a much better understanding and appreciation for marketing. That's fantastic, and I want you to keep the momentum going. While my ACTION system is easy to follow, once things are going, you must INVEST in your marketing.

Let's define an investment: spending money or capital in order to gain profitable returns. So when you spend money on marketing, what do you expect to get in return? Those returns are probably in the form of short-term gains such as new sales, new customers, signups, etc. Or they may be long-term goals such as brand awareness, which in turn makes it easier to sell later and keep repeat customers. The point is that we spend money on marketing in order to get something in return, just like the definition of an investment. For example, you don't spend money on redoing your website because it makes you feel good. You would spend that money because it's going to persuade more customers to do business with you, providing you with a return on your investment.

If your long lost cousin were to bequeath you $100,000 upon his death with the only requirement that you spend it on marketing in the next 30 days, how would you use it? What would you do? Of course, the smartest decision would be to hire me to get it done for you, but play along for now if you will.

Let's say you're in Las Vegas and each of the different games represents a different type of marketing.

- There's craps - let's say that's print advertising.
- There's roulette - let's say that's content marketing.
- There's slots - let's say that's social media marketing.
- There's poker - let's say that's pay-per-click (PPC).

So many games aka marketing options! Where would you put your money - this windfall you just received? Would you split it up over the 30 days? Or place all your bets on a single day? Would you try a few things, and if they didn't work, would you take more risk? Would you double down if you were winning? Would you put it all on the table if you weren't?

How are you going to roll the dice with those marketing dollars?

That's the problem. When it comes to marketing, those who don't follow the ACTION system are just gambling. They're rolling the dice and hoping for a win, usually a big one. It rarely happens. Remember, when it comes to gambling, the odds are not in your favor. It's the house that wins, not you. That's true in Vegas, and it's true in the world of marketing.

However, let's be very clear right now: Investing is ***not*** gambling.

Investing is making smart decisions on where you're spending your time, effort, and money on your marketing efforts. It's not about cost, it's about ROI. It's about knowing, "If I spend $X on this, I can expect to get $X+++ in return." But that's where small business owners get stuck: the spending part.

Here's how I've seen small business owners approach "the spending money part of marketing," depending on where they are in their growth cycle.

There's the business owner who looks at it as an ***expense***, a low priority effort, an unnecessary cost. Usually, they're in survival mode.

There's the business owner who is reluctant to invest in anything at all until they know a particular strategy will work. They don't know how much is appropriate to invest; therefore, they can't make a budgetary decision on whether or not to move forward, so they don't. The result is a perpetual cycle of non-investment.

There's the business owner who thinks it's risky to invest in a certain type of marketing that they've never done before. "Digital marketing? I heard another guy put all his marketing dollars into Facebook advertising and didn't get anything out of it. I'm not taking that chance."

> Marketing is an investment in your business. It is not a line item on your expense report.

There's the business owner who understands that they need to market, but has no idea what to do. Remember spaghetti marketing? Those small business owners are throwing spaghetti at the wall, throwing money at anything they ***think*** will bring more business. One day it's PPC, one day it's content marketing, one day it's mailing out postcards. They spend foolishly to see if anything sticks.

There's the business owner who is in growth mode: Things are good, everyone is busy, so why bother with the expense and hassle? They forget about marketing. Things slide. The marketing stops. They become complacent. If you're following the lessons and putting the ACTION system into action (pun intended), at this stage, this could be you. You're getting results. You've done the right things to find your target market, leads are coming in, and you're converting them into sales. When things are good, it's easy to get into a comfort zone and stick with the way things are. Don't do that! Remember, the acronym is not ACT, it's ACTION. There's a reason for that, so make sure you finish reading the entire book. If you stop following the ACTION system when revenue starts flowing, I assure you, it will not ***continue*** to flow.

No matter where you are in your business growth cycle, you need to be marketing. What is going to differentiate you from the others is that you're using the ACTION system to make smart marketing decisions to grow your business in a systematic and manageable way. Investing in your marketing allows you to leverage what's working while testing out new methods and strategies. You grow as far and as fast as you want. The difference? You're controlling the decisions and using data to help move your business forward.

Expense vs. Investment

You've no doubt heard the saying, "In order to make money, you need to spend money." The key is to make sure you're spending it wisely. That's what the "I" in the ACTION system is about.

It's about INVESTING in your marketing to get a ***return on your investment***.

I can't tell you how many times I'm asked, "Stacey, how much should I spend on marketing?" "What should my marketing budget be?"

That's the million-dollar question.

But I do have an answer.

It doesn't matter how much you ***spend*** on marketing. What matters is your ROI on whatever you do spend. That's the only metric that matters. When you know you'll make $X+++ when you invest $X in your marketing, you'll be much more excited to do it, confident of what your results will be.

In my coffee and smoothie business, I invest in PPC advertising. I know from implementing the ACTION system that people who are actively looking for a coffee or smoothie bar use Google to search for this type of catering service.

Advertising my catering services on Google is not cheap. I pay between $6 and $10 per click on Google AdWords. That's just for one ***click***. If a prospect clicks to go to my website and then leaves without taking an action, that's $6 to $10 down the drain. But I happily pay Google hundreds of dollars every month for those clicks because they convert. Sure it may cost $6 to 10 for a click, but my average catering job is worth over $500. I'm willing to invest in AdWords because there's a consistent positive ROI.

Would you invest $10 to make a $500 sale? Heck yeah, you would! You'd turn on the faucet and let the business pour in.

When it comes to PPC or any type of marketing, most small business owners get scared away. They view it as an expense. In their eyes, it's a line item expenditure - something that has to be paid, like rent or a utility bill. Their language is, "What is it going to ***cost***?"

That's the wrong question. Instead ask, ***"What is the ROI?"***

When you base your marketing decisions on ROI, you're able to defend and appreciate the money you spend on any initiative.

Think of ROI as the quantitative benefit (aka revenue) you receive above and beyond your original payment. For example, if you pay $1,000 a month for marketing services and you earn $1,500 in new revenue from those services, your ROI is $500.

There are a lot of marketing metrics you can measure in your business... and maybe that will be the subject of my next book. The key is not to get caught up in vanity metrics. What do I mean by that?

Vanity metrics are metrics that make you feel good but really do nothing for your bottom line and the success of your business. For example, gross sales. There are a lot of snake-oil-peddling marketing "gurus" out there peddling claims like, "I can make your business $100,000 in sales in the next 30 days. Just 'invest' in my program for $1,000."

What they're not telling you is that 1) they've never done it themselves, and 2) they spent $200,000 to make the $100,000. Don't believe their magic voodoo. Do the math: They just lost $100,000! I'm the smelling salt you need to keep you away from those peddlers.

Plaster this quote on the wall in front of you, so look at it every day:

"Gross is for vanity. Net is for sanity."

You'll sleep a lot better at night and your bank account will be much healthier when you focus on the metrics that matter.

> Metrics matters, but you must only focus on the ones that will drive your business and your profitability.

There so many other vanity metrics in which you can get caught up, spinning your wheels, if you aren't careful. For example, social media tends to focus on how many likes you have. Look, you can't deposit likes in the bank. That's not a metric on which you should focus. Or email… it's easy to get caught up in the deliverability rate, opens, clicks. Those are vanity metrics because they make you feel good when "people see your stuff." Yes, those metrics have some merit in building your brand and creating recognition, but like I said, you can't deposit those in the bank, so those cannot be your sole focus. Sure, they might make you feel good, but feeling good and profitability are not the same. Stay focused on the metrics that truly impact your bottom line.

Lifetime Value

There are a lot of metrics that you can be measuring. Like I said, the number of leads, dollars sold, "break even" all matter, but only one matters the most: customer lifetime value. It's one of the most overlooked and least understood metrics in business - even though it's one of the easiest to figure out. Plus it's the one that will help you grow your business and boost your bottom line.

Why is this particular metric so important? It will help you know how much repeat business you can expect from a particular customer, which in turn will help you decide how much you're willing to spend to "buy" or acquire that customer in the first place. Once you know how frequently a customer buys and how much they spend, you'll then be in a much better position to determine how to allocate your resources to retain that customer and keep them happy.

Customer lifetime value measures the profit your business makes from those repeat customers, clients, or patients. It helps you answer questions such as:

- Marketing: How much should I spend to acquire a customer?
- Product: How can I offer products and services tailored for my ***best*** customers?
- Customer support: How much should I spend to service and retain a customer?
- Sales: What types of customers should sales reps spend the most time trying to acquire?

The easiest way to calculate customer lifetime value is to take the revenue you earn from a customer and subtract the money spent on acquiring and serving them.

Use this formula:

(Average Value of a Sale) x (Number of Repeat Transactions) x (Average Retention Time in Months or Years for a Typical Customer)

For example, let's say you own a gym. The lifetime value of a customer who spends $20 every month for three years would be:

$20 x 12 months x 3 years = $720 in total revenue ($240 per year)

Now you can see why many gyms offer a free starter membership to drive traffic. Gym owners know that as long as they spend less than $240 to acquire a new member, the customer will prove profitable in a short amount of time.

P.T. Barnum, the founder of Barnum & Bailey Circus, once said: "Without promotion something terrible happens. Nothing."

Without promotion, it's difficult to maintain the status quo and almost impossible to sustain growth. Investing in your marketing is what will keep your business alive and allow it to thrive and grow.

Too Much?

Okay, okay. I've made my point and you understand why you need to invest in your marketing. But is it possible to invest too much at the outset? It is. It's not that investing a large amount of time and effort in your marketing is a gamble. Instead, the risk comes from investing too heavily before you know your ideal strategy. Remember the analogy of getting a windfall of $100,000 and heading to Vegas? If you spent it all in one day without learning the nuances of the various games, you're really gambling! Starting with a smaller marketing investment gives you time to gather information about your target market and what the potential results might be. By doing this, you can be more effective when you scale up your investment.

Marketing results tend to unfold in a curve. I tell my clients that marketing is a long-term game. They may not see immediate results. It can easily take six months or longer to understand your target market, test different messages, and dominate a media.

Here's what the "other marketing guys" won't tell you because it involves some tough love, but I'm here to help you implement the ACTION system, so you can become a #SmallBizMarketingWiz: Early in your marketing efforts, you won't see much of a return on your investment. However, because you are doing the right marketing to the right market at the right time in the right media, your ROI will increase as you spend more time and energy on it.

As entrepreneurs, we want fast results, we want it all now. You have to be patient to see the results you want. When it comes to investing in your marketing, I coach my clients that it's better to start small and maintain and build as the strategy develops.

DIY

When it comes to investing in marketing, how you invest in your marketing also matters.

Let's say you want to redo the bathroom in your house. You're going to "invest" in fixing it up.

You can ***do it yourself*** - buy books or watch videos on all of the different aspects of renovating your bathroom. It's going to take you a long time and you're going to make a lot of mistakes because you don't have the expertise you need in all aspects of renovation. Sure, you can probably install a faucet and paint the walls, but are you the best person to do the electrical work, the plumbing, the tiling, and every other aspect involved in a bathroom renovation? Probably not. DIY may seem to be the least expensive "investment," but you'll ultimately end up wasting time and spending more to fix the messes you created by not doing it right in the first place.

Another option is to ***do it with some help***. Maybe you know how to handle some aspects of a bathroom renovation, but you'll leave the more complicated pieces to a professional. This is a better option, but it won't be the fastest nor the cheapest. Because the renovation has to be completed in a certain order - you can't paint the walls until everything else is done - it's going to slow the process down. You may do some things and then bring in someone to do other pieces, but you've got to schedule them, coordinate efforts, pay for each part of the project. You effectively take on the role of contractor, and any good contractor will tell you that finding and coordinating the subcontractors can be the most challenging part of the job. Unless you're a really great contractor, there will be no consistency in getting the different pieces of the project done. The

> Do what you do best; outsource the rest.

project will get done - eventually - but you'll look back wishing you had "invested" in a better solution.

The best option is to ***do what you do best, outsource the rest.*** This will generate the fastest results without taking your valuable time. You'd "invest" in a contractor or company that is an expert in bathroom renovations. They'll know exactly what to do and how to do it, they'll have the right tools and people in place to get it done, and they'll get it done efficiently - and won't leave you a mess to clean up. Sure it may seem to "cost" more, but your time is freed up to do what you do best, and you're getting exactly what you wanted - a beautiful working bathroom completed quickly and efficiently, the benefit of which you'll get to enjoy for a very long time.

When it comes to investing in your marketing - just as in renovating your bathroom - there are different levels at which you can do that. It depends on how fast and how far you want to grow. Which investment do you think will get you the results you're looking to achieve?

Take the time, money, and resources to invest in your marketing. That means being in it for the long haul. You want a return on your investment. That doesn't necessarily mean today or tomorrow. That means over time.

At the end of the day, marketing will show up on your financial statements as an expense, there's no way to get around that, but hopefully you now understand that marketing really is an investment - not a cost - that will help your business grow and achieve your goals.

Get It Done the EZ Way:

- You need to invest in marketing once revenues start flowing in… or they'll stop in a hurry.
- An investment is something for which you spend $X and anticipate getting $X+++ in return.
- If you fail to follow the ACTION system, you are gambling with your marketing dollars. (Hint: As in Vegas, the house always wins.)
- Do not think of marketing dollars spent as a cost. Those dollars are an investment in your business.
- Never ask, "What is the cost?" Always ask, "What is the ROI?"
- Beware the vanity metrics and stay focused on the ones that will truly impact your business, profitability, and bank account.
- "Gross is for vanity. Net is for sanity."
- When you understand what your customers' lifetime value is, you will be able to more accurately answer the

critical questions about how to market and run your business.

- You actually can spend too much on marketing too early. Take time to test and figure out where you will get the greatest ROI.
- DIYing it doesn't usually work to well with bathroom renovations, and the same is true of DIY marketing. Focus on what you do best and outsource the rest!

EZ-er Way: Contact The Small Biz Marketing Specialist! smallbizmarketingspecialist.com

Chapter Eight:

Ongoing

Know what happens if you put a frog in a pot of boiling water? Of course, he'll jump right out. But if you put that frog in water and slowly turn up the heat, he'll boil to death. The incremental change toward a dangerous situation doesn't register. I don't want you to be placed in boiling water or to boil to death, so let's talk about the next part of the ACTION system.

The "O" in the ACTION system is about ensuring your marketing is ONGOING. It's about doing something every day to move your business forward.

Unfortunately, I see a lot of small business owners who are like the frog and end up on either side of the spectrum: They feel they have to do ***a lot of things*** to keeping their marketing going (i.e., they put themselves in boiling water) or ***they become complacent and don't do anything*** (i.e., they don't realize the water is getting slowly but dangerously hotter).

Both are bad options because there is no consistency. You don't want to be the frog that jumps from one marketing tactic to another when you feel the heat. You also don't want to be the frog that, because you weren't doing anything all along, one day wakes up to find he's in hot water - literally.

When things are going well in your business, it's easy to become complacent. Leads are coming in, customers are buying and returning to buy more, money is in the bank. The marketing is working. You're in your "happy place." The problem is you've found your comfort zone and you're sticking with it. But "business happens." Google changes its rules, and as a result, now you're not showing up in searches. Gmail decides to send all of your emails to the promotions tab, so now no one is seeing them. Facebook bans your account because you ran a contest they didn't like. Word of mouth is how you've gotten most of your business until this point, but that referral network is drying up. It happens every day. You don't want to find yourself stuck because you were complacent without a strategy in place to market on an ongoing basis.

> Don't be like the frog. Don't hop around and don't get complacent.

Too many small business owners fall into complacency. Your business isn't bleeding cash, you're making money, more would be nice - but who has the time to do more marketing? Besides you've got a business to run, you've got an underperforming employee to deal with, vendors are clamoring to get paid, and the computers are on the fritz. There are worse things in life than not marketing after all, right?

Let me be clear: Marketing complacency sucks! It's not good for your business, your employees, your bottom line, or you. If you're complacent about marketing, you will go broke. Growth is the only way to sustain and increase profits, and marketing is the key to unlocking that growth. If you want more money, you cannot be satisfied with the status quo. Since money isn't going to grow on trees or fall from the sky, you're going to have to do something about it. You already know what I'm going to say, right? You need to get into ACTION!

Don't worry and don't put down this book because ***I'm going to make it easy for you and tell you exactly what to do next***. But before I do, I want to address the biggest hindrance small business owners face when it comes to making their marketing an ongoing activity. It's even worse than complacency.

It's not that you don't know that you ***should*** have ongoing marketing. You understand that marketing is an ongoing activity. You actually get so excited about it that you just want to know everything you can about it. I can see the glimmer and excitement in your eyes. There are so many options available to you today - online and offline - you tell yourself ongoing marketing will be no problem.

Option Overload

But then you have to decide what you're going to do and how you're going to keep at it.

When it comes to all of the different marketing strategies available to you, it's like looking at all of the shiny pieces of jewelry in the showcase. They glimmer, shine, and call out to you, "Buy ***me***, I'm shiny!" It's called shiny object syndrome, and small business owners are notorious for being diagnosed with it. You bounce from this to that to the other thing with too much damn excitement. That shiny object syndrome can be hard to resist.

Is this you? It's okay to admit it because I'm guilty of this too from time to time. It's times like these when I have to become my own therapist, smack my own head and say, "NO! NO! NO!"

We live in a world of option overload. So many choices, so little time. This is what happens when there are so many ideas that you want to try them all, so you hop from one idea to the next. It always feels like the newest idea is going to be great. The newest idea is going to solve every problem. We find a new technique, new software, new tools, and we chase after them. The start of something is always exciting because it holds the promise of success. It's what we've been waiting for - the new idea or tool - so we have to do it or have it.

With shiny object syndrome, you might be able to start a hundred projects, but you won't follow through with any of them. Sure, you dive in and do some activities, but you end up getting about halfway done and then something new will come along – or a fire in your business needs to be put out – and off you go again.

The problem with so many options is that it can cause you to go down the wrong path and end up preventing you from actually accomplishing anything at all. It's a lack of attention and focus that can derail your business if you're not careful. When you're chasing the newest idea, you're not spending time on your business. You're not focusing on the things that matter to build the business you always dreamed you'd have.

> Beware shiny object syndrome! It can derail your efforts and unravel your plan.

You can get caught up in information overload, too – just like you can with shiny object syndrome. How many books, courses, and programs have you purchased? How many did you actually finish? Of those, how many did you actually ***do something*** with – how many ideas did you actually implement? You see, you can have a bookshelf and computer full of the latest and greatest marketing strategies, but if you don't implement and put them into action, it's a complete waste of time and money. What you've become is a jack of all trades and a master of none.

Just Do Something

You can stop all of these situations from happening. You can win the complacency and shiny object syndrome battle.

Do something every day to move your business forward. ***Something.*** Not lots of things. Not just one thing. ***Something.***

It's at this point in the book that for many the light bulb goes off. "Yes, I get it! I know I need to not only do marketing, but do it consistently. ONGOING. Yes!"

Then they pick up the phone or send me an email because they realize they need to ***do what they do best and outsource the rest.*** They know their time, effort, and expertise are better spent doing other things in their businesses. They know that while, sure, they may do some marketing today or tomorrow, it's the ongoing, regular, consistency that will bring them the best results.

Can you do it yourself? Absolutely. That's why I say do ***something***. One thing each day that will move your business forward. What it shouldn't be is spending time on social media, posting about what you ate for dinner last night. Nor should it be spending hours figuring out how to automate your lead generation campaign in your CRM if you don't have the tech skills to do it.

In the Resources section, I give you a marketing plan based on whether you're new, intermediate, or advanced when it comes to marketing. These are the activities you should be spending your time and effort on if you want to do the marketing yourself.

Please be realistic with yourself. If you tend to get complacent and freeze when it comes to getting your marketing done... or if you're on the other end of the spectrum where you're doing too many things and easily finding yourself sucked into another shiny object, contact me immediately. I'll put together the perfect marketing plan based on how far and fast you want to grow, and my team will get it done - every day, ongoing.

Magic Marketing Pill

When you're not feeling well, you go to the doctor, and most might shove you out the door and say, "Take this pill." The same thing happens to many small business owners with their marketing. They regard marketing as a pill to take when something is wrong. "Not enough customers? Take some marketing and call me in the morning. Oh and don't forget to leave your payment at the door before you leave."

The problem is that what you're really looking for is a magic pill… the elusive magic marketing pill. The magical formula for quick sales, a powerhouse brand, and five-star reviews. The one thing that can change everything. We cry to the heavens with outstretched arms, "What is it?"

When you see a diet pill that promises washboard abs in 30 days, do you believe it? We all want to believe it will work because we want to push that button and get a silver-bullet solution. But deep down I'm sure you don't really believe for one second that there is a pill that will remove body fat and replace it with muscle without any other lifestyle changes.

But what happens when you see a marketing tactic that promises to solve all your sales problems in a few months? Do you believe ***that***? Unfortunately many business owners do!

> There is no magic pill. You have to take ACTION!

The search for a marketing magic pill has led too many entrepreneurs to spend millions of dollars on websites, pay-per-click advertising, print ads, radio commercials, and the "next big thing" usually with lackluster results. Too many businesses have literally thrown money away in this maddening search for the short, easy way to high sales. Just "swallow the pill," sit back, and expect a windfall of sales.

Marketing is not a pill. It's the food that nourishes your business and gives it the energy and sustenance to get your business to where you want it to go. You need it throughout the day, every day. It's a holistic approach that is implemented effectively over a long period of time. When you consistently reach out to customers, attract their attention, and pique their interest in creative and thoughtful ways, you will begin to get the traction your business needs.

Feed Your Business

As you know, there's food that's good for you and food that's not so good for you. It's important that you're nourishing and investing in what will give your business the most strength. In general, good in = good out.

Here's how you nourish your business and put a process in place to make marketing an ongoing activity:

Start with a budget. Don't have one? That's a huge red flag. It's time to develop one. Yes, that may mean more meetings and feel like it's pulling teeth in deciding what may need to go in order to have marketing funds, but if your business is to survive and thrive, you need to market it.

Create a marketing plan. If I sat down with you today and said, "So, where's your marketing plan for this year? What are you doing to grow and how will you implement the ideas and strategies?," you may pull out a long document, complete with graphics and charts - or you may have nothing at all. You've been busy. You'll list a few excuses, then you'll say, "Well, I should probably get on that." Yes, you should! You have to. The longer you wait, the more behind the curve you'll be.

Stop playing the blame game. You know, sales blames marketing that they have no leads; marketing blames sales that there's no business coming in. Hey, we can play the blame game all day long - but at the end of the day, we know who is really responsible for the growth of your business... and it's not your sales team. In fact, the fact that you're not marketing regularly (aka "ongoing") is probably driving your sales team nuts, and you're lucky to still have them closing any deals for you. Believe me, I promise you that your sales team (specifically if their compensation is commission based) wants nothing more than to close more leads for your business. Putting that burden squarely on the sales team's shoulders is just a way to try to shift the responsibility. If you're not actively marketing every day and assisting your sales team in generating new leads, you'll never grow your business.

Marketing Is a Marathon

ONGOING marketing is about focusing on the fundamentals.

With your diet, you know that the fundamentals of losing weight and being healthier are to eat right and exercise. If you consistently eat healthy foods and exercise on a regular basis, then you'll naturally lose fat and build more muscle. No pills required.

With your marketing, it's essentially the same formula. Consistently improve on the fundamentals. When clients come to me for help in getting their marketing done, I only focus on five fundamentals:

1. Social media
2. Content
3. Email
4. Direct mail
5. Reputation management

If you focus on just these five things and do them regularly and consistently, you'll have a vibrant business.

Here's the problem: Most never do ***anything*** about it.

The biggest hurdle to marketing success is taking the first step. "Wanting to do it" isn't the same as "doing it."

Marketing is a marathon. It's the long run. It's not a sprint.

If you're going to run a marathon and you've never done it before, are you going to just slip on your sneakers and run 26.2 miles? I doubt it. Chances are the ambulance will be picking you up very close to where you started.

Whether you're training for a marathon or training to make your marketing a long-term view, you need to start small. I mean, really small.

Don't decide to "do social media" and start posting on Facebook, Twitter, LinkedIn, Pinterest, YouTube, Instagram, and Snapchat. That's too much, and you'll probably just end up frustrated and deflated.

> In the race toward successful marketing and profitability, be ready for a marathon.

Instead, do one small thing. Pick the social media platform that will most resonate with your target audience. Do one thing each day to get better at it. Look at your insights to see what's working and what's not. You'll find that with each small step you gain confidence, you gain strength, it becomes easier. One step in front of the other, day after day, and then suddenly you realize, "I just ran a mile." So you're posting regularly and people are starting to share your content. "I just ran five miles." You're ready to use the platform to reach more people by live streaming. "I just passed the 15-mile marker." It's time to add another platform, and you know you still have more that can be done, but you'll get there. Suddenly, reaching the 26-mile mark doesn't seem impossible, and the finish line starts to come into view.

When your marketing starts taking off and you're starting to see some traction (aka you're at the five-mile marker), it's tempting to want to do more (aka run another mile). Doing so is fine, as long as you know that you can maintain your pace. However, since chances are you're not going to be capable of running full-speed for the entire race, know where to push and where to conserve energy. To keep your momentum going, break your marketing into smaller, more manageable chunks. Set goals for daily, weekly and monthly targets. You'll feel much more motivated to continue achieving them when you're making progress.

It's not so much the starting of your marketing that hinders success, it's the consistency. Relating back to the marathon, when you're in the final stretch, your muscles are burning, you're tired, and the only thing keeping you going is willpower. This is where everything you've been doing so far, all of the training, all of the healthy food you've been eating, really kicks in. All of those goals you set months ago to keep you motivated and all the training you've done are paying off.

The final part of the run is a test of your endurance, much like marketing.

You can post a blog or a podcast, receive a few likes and no comments, and scream that marketing does not work for you. But marketing "is a marathon, not a sprint." It takes time and energy to build your customer base.

Making a commitment to run 26.2 miles is a big deal and requires consistency and persistency. Training occurs over months, not days, and requires countless hours of preparation. Running a marathon doesn't happen overnight. Neither does successful marketing.

Take your time. Make marketing an ongoing activity. You'll cross the finish line a winner!

Get It Done the EZ Way:

- Don't be the frog – either bouncing from boiling pot to boiling pot or so complacent that you fail to realize it's getting dangerously hot.
- It's easy to become complacent about marketing when things are going well, but honestly, marketing complacency sucks and will lead to going broke.
- Beware of "shiny object syndrome" in which the latest, new thing gets your attention and derails your focus.

- Shiny object syndrome and information overload can lead you to start a hundred things, but you'll wind up implementing zero.
- Overcome shiny object syndrome by doing something - one thing each day that will move your business forward.
- There is no magic marketing pill just as there is no magic weight loss pill. Results take effort.
- Marketing is a marathon. You can't train for a 26.2-mile race in a day, a week, or a month. You train for the long haul. The same is true for your marketing efforts.

EZ-er Way: Contact The Small Biz Marketing Specialist! *smallbizmarketingspecialist.com*

Ongoing

Chapter Nine:

Nurture

If you've been implementing the ACTION system so far, you have the foundational pieces in place to attract the right people at the right time using the right media. You're using metrics to make the right decisions, and you're marketing every day.

You might think you could stop at this point; however, there's still one missing piece, and it's the piece that's the most important... the one that ties everything you've built so far into a well-oiled machine. Now you must create a culture of WOW! moments - creating consistent, memorable, and delightful experiences that make customers, clients, or patients want to stick with you for life.

So we're at the "N" in the ACTION system. The "N" in the ACTION system is about ***nurturing*** those customers, clients, or patients, so they bond to you like glue, come back again and again with open wallets, leave rave reviews, refer others, and become brand ambassadors. It's the part of the ACTION system in which you should spend your greatest time and effort when it comes to your marketing initiatives.

My parents have been married for over 50 years. My dad probably didn't realize it at the time but he used the ACTION system to keep their marriage strong. He got my mom's the attention. He connected. He built transactions that led up to a "Will you marry me?" He invested in the relationship by "never stop dating" (actually that was my mom's advice) and even today they still have date nights. Building their relationship together is ongoing. Everyone asks my parents how they've managed to stay in love together for so long, and as I shared earlier, my dad always answers, "It's cheaper to keep 'er."

Now you may laugh, but it's actually true. It ***is*** cheaper to keep 'er... and that's what nurture is all about.

Did you know it costs five times more to attract a new customer than to keep an existing one? Worse than that, it costs 16 times more to bring a new customer up to the same level as a current one! Why then do so many small business owners focus more time and effort on getting the ***new*** sale versus keeping the customer, client, or patient they already have? (The quick answer: Because they're not reading this book like you are, and if that's what you've been doing, it's time to change that strategy!)

Let them waste their time, effort, and money chasing the new leads and prospects. Here are a few cited statistics that drive home the importance of focusing on the ones you've already won:

- 80% of your future profits will come from just 20% of your existing customers. (Small Biz Trends)
- 65% of a company's business comes from existing customers. (Small Biz Trends)
- 50% of consumers use a company more frequently after a positive customer experience. (NewVoice)
- Loyal customers are five times as likely to repurchase, five times as likely to forgive, four times as likely to refer, and seven times as likely to try a new offering. (Temkin Group)
- Increasing customer retention rates by 5% increases profits by 25% to 95%. (Harvard Business School)

You've already spent the time, effort, and money to build that important "know, like, and trust" factor. If "Dan" has never done business with you and "Jane" has, who do you think will increase your bank balance faster?

When small business owners approach me to help with their marketing, I ask them what they think their biggest problem is. The majority say, "Getting more customers." I tell them I can definitely help them with that, and suggest they're already sitting on a pot of gold. "Would you like my help in cashing it in?"

Of course they say, "Yes! Let's get more new customers."

I then tell them, "No, it's not more ***new*** customers you need – at least not now. You're sitting on a pot of gold which consists of your current and/or former customers, clients, or patients. It's your low-hanging fruit."

> Retention beats acquisition every time!

Imagine you're a fruit picker in an orchard. The low-hanging fruit is easy to reach, and you can often pick those pieces easily and quickly as you walk through the orchard. However, if you wanted to reach the fruit higher up on the trees, you would have to drag a ladder from tree to tree – more effort and more time. Focusing your marketing efforts on the low-hanging stuff is often the thing most likely to produce quick wins. Low-hanging fruit is exactly what it sounds like: It's the ripe, delicious, easy-to-access opportunity that requires little effort to harvest. (And this book is all about being easy, right?)

The Quick and EZ Solution

Many small business owners look at a problem and try to find some "shiny object" solution when the simplest route - the one that will provide fairly instantaneous results - is the one right within their doors (or their database). Too many small business owners skip over these "acres of diamonds in their backyard" and go looking for much harder-to-find prey or drag that proverbial ladder around the orchard to access the fruit that's harder to reach.

For example, many entrepreneurs pay for expensive - and hard to track - brand advertising of their businesses when it would be much more effective and less costly to spend resources in getting new customers through referrals from current customers. Picking the low-hanging fruit - those customers and sales that are easy to harvest and convert - will allow your business to make quick gains. It will boost your confidence. It will put more profit in the bank that can then be used to develop more expensive, longer-term customer acquisition strategies. It's the #1 strategy I recommend to small business owners who want to quickly ramp up their marketing, whether they work with me or not.

When you have customers, clients, or patients who are highly engaged with your company, they'll be more open to upsell opportunities and more likely to try a new product or service. They're also less price-sensitive and will spend more money with you each year. Even better, they're much more likely to become brand ambassadors and advocate your brand to acquaintances and colleagues.

In my coffee and smoothie business, I really don't have to do a lot of marketing to get new business. I have a solid client base who I nurture, so they come back again and again, leave me rave reviews, and refer others. They are my marketing team. How would your business change if your customers, clients, or patients became your marketing team?

My nurture program is simple and inexpensive. It consists of a handwritten note after each event, emailing some pictures of the happy people enjoying their drinks, tagging them on social media, mailing a quarterly printed newsletter, emailing about every six weeks with a new-client-only special, and sending fun little gifts twice a year. If a client hasn't contacted us within six months to come back for another job, we reach out directly. One out of every three re-book.

These clients come back again and again because they already "know, like, and trust" us. Price is rarely an issue. It's much easier to upsell them to a larger cup size or additional add-ons because they know they'll love it. Considering 42 percent of my catering clients are repeat customers and represent more than six-figures of income, yeah, it's well worth making sure I nurture them!

Whose Job Is It?

It's important to reach out to your customers, clients, or patients on a regular basis, so you stay front-of-mind. Remember, it's not their job to remember to do business with you!

I used to go to a local bakery. They had delectable breads, desserts, gelato. I would try something new every time I went. Every month or so, I'd get a large postcard in the mail that had some fun trivia facts about a product they were featuring and there'd be an incentive to come in. The cards were personalized, and they remembered what I got last time and invited me to try the new item or two they just introduced. I went there every single time I received that postcard in the mail. It "reminded" me to do business with them, not the other way around. But then....

The postcards stopped coming. I stopped going there. I hadn't even realized it until one day I drove by the store and said to myself, "I haven't been there in a long time. I don't remember them sending me any of those great postcards recently." Since I love connecting with small business owners, I stopped in and started talking to the owner. I mentioned to him that I hadn't received a postcard recently and asked if I was still on the mailing list. He said, "No, I stopped sending those postcards. Now it's on an app."

Bad decision on his part. My guess is he was looking at the cost of sending out those postcards, and some new-age tech company sold him on "going to an app because everyone's on their phones and no one reads mail anymore."

Well he lost my business because he broke a cardinal marketing rule: It's not my job to remember to do business with you. It's your job as a business owner to remind me - and give me a reason - to come back. Those postcards reminded me to come back. The app doesn't. The app may trigger an email, but my inbox is overloaded, so that's easy to overlook. A post card in my mailbox stands out.

Reality is you're not going to be able to keep every customer, client, or patient you get. There will always be some churn. People move, their tastes change, they even die. Those are things you can't control. What you can control is minimizing the holes in your leaky bucket.

> It's not your customer's job to remember you. It's your job to be memorable.

What's a leaky bucket? Imagine a bucket, and your customers, clients, or patients are the water. In the beginning, you fill that bucket with water (customers, clients, or patients). You spend all of your time focusing on filling the bucket. What you don't realize is that over time, the bucket starts to rust and leak. At first, it's just a small drip here and there. Then the hole gets a little bigger and some other holes start forming. Eventually there are a lot of holes in the bucket, and the water is leaking out quickly. By this time, it's usually months or years later and the business owner is scratching their head, wondering where all of their business is going.

Yes, you need to focus on filling your bucket with water. More importantly, you need to plug those leaks. When you do, you'll not only have a stronger customer, client or patient base, you'll have a stronger bank balance to show for it.

Creating WOWs!

Think about the last time you were completely impressed by a company. You probably did business with them more than once and maybe even told a few of your friends about your experience. You may have posted about it on social media and left a raving review. To make the nurture part of your marketing plan really work, you need to start with creating WOW! moments.

A WOW! moment is an experience that leaves a lasting impression on your customers, clients, or patients. I like to think of it as scripting smiles along the customer journey. It's the smaller interactions - the "little things" - that make people remember you. Wowing your customers involves going the extra mile to create a memorable, delightful experience that will create customers, clients, or patients for life.

The first step in wowing your customers involves delivering more than what you promised. This may seem simple and obvious, but in the hustle and bustle of daily work, it's so often overlooked. Here are some examples to show you how easy creating WOW! moments can be:

- An art gallery could allow a prospective buyer to "try it before you buy it," so they could take the piece home to see how it looks.
- A dessert shop could have special VIP events where brand evangelists get to try new products and get special discounts and giveaways.
- A landscaping company could email or mail tips to keep the yard looking its best between cuts.
- A clothing boutique has a "red carpet area" and takes pictures of customers in their new outfits.

These WOW! moments don't cost a lot of money. They don't take a lot of time or effort to implement. Yet they make a ***huge*** difference in making customers, clients, or patients feel special. So few companies do anything to create experiences that excite and delight. It's the one differentiator that can have the biggest impact on your business. The funny thing is, once you start incorporating these WOW!

moments into your culture, you'll find you want to do it over and over again. Don't be surprised if your customers, clients, or patients start WOWing you.

This happens all the time in my coffee and smoothie business. My clients email me immediately after an event - even before I've had a chance to ask how the event went - raving about how much they loved it, how everyone complimented them on putting together such a great event, and they post and tag us in pictures online. They tip their servers very generously, which of course then motivates my team to work even harder. It's a wonderful cycle.

In my marketing business, I truly have the best clients! They send ***me*** gifts… isn't it supposed to be the other way around? I get handwritten cards, books, food. I am so blessed to have them in my life. While most other marketing agencies treat their clients as a "business relationship," I have a strong personal bond with many of mine. They invite me to stay in their homes. We get together when I travel to their cities. I know their families. I know them as a person. Sure we talk business, but we also have an incredibly strong personal bond. I have a client who called me because she needed a crying shoulder when she found out she may have a serious medical condition. I also have a client who sent both of my kids graduation presents. One client brought his whole family to Washington, D.C., so he could personally meet "Small Business Stacey"! (Yes, he also wanted to see the area, but he booked his trip around my being in town so we could connect). There's a special bond there that goes well beyond "just doing business together." That's the magic of incorporating NURTURE into your business and your life.

Six Simple Words

There are two types of experiences you'll remember most:

- Those that are "bad."
- Those that are "great."

You know what each is. You can see that experience in your mind. You can remember how you felt and how you reacted. Unfortunately today, most companies are somewhere in between these extremes - stuck in mediocrity. That may be the worst place of all. I want you to commit today to not being stuck in the middle. Do something nice for someone today - a random act of kindness - and build on that one customer at a time.

What you'll find is that once you've built a culture of creating these WOW! moments, it's much easier to offer your customers, clients, or patients more. Sure offering more can mean "selling more," but it also means "giving more." Ask yourself, "How can I help my customers, clients, or patients today and in the future?" The solution doesn't have to be your specific product or service, nor does it have to result in a sale.

Helping can be as simple as providing tips and resources related to their inquiries and/or what they're most interested in. Here are three ways to tactfully increase your revenue while continuing to be helpful:

- Cross-sell: Customers aren't always aware of the perfect product or service pairings and may be willing to purchase related items that enhance their experience.
- Upsell: Listen to your customers and try to understand their needs. They might be willing to pay extra for special treatment, warranties, or monthly programs.
- New products: Remember to help your customers by identifying things that will enhance their lives by notifying them of new products or services.

There are six words you can use to make more money from the customers, clients, or patients who already know, like, and trust you:

"Would you like fries with that?"

They're the same six words McDonald's uses to scale its business and sell nine million pounds of fries every day. But McDonald's just doesn't stop at asking their customers if they want fries, they continually take it one step further by asking if they want a drink or a larger sized drink. These incremental sales do wonders in helping them boost their bottom line and contributed to their more than $23 billion in revenue the company made last year.

What if you were to ask this question to your customers, clients, or patients, changing "fries" for whatever products or services you sell? Would it add immediate dollars to your bottom line? Absolutely.

I'm sure most small business owners understand this principle and know all-too-well the ol' "Would you like fries with that," but I don't understand then why so many small business owners are leaving money on the table. I don't want you to be in that group.

> Don't leave money on the table: Offer the fries!

I was speaking at an event in Indianapolis and had to check out the local small business scene. After all, I am the Small Biz Marketing Specialist. Walking around the city, I came across a women's clothing boutique. The window display had an eclectic mix of fun/casual clothing, footwear, and several collectibles. It caught my attention and made the grade enough for me to want to see more. I entered the store.

I was greeted by a woman who was wearing a brightly embroidered jacket with jeans similar to the ones I had noticed in the window. She said, "Welcome. Is this your first time visiting Marigold?" I told her it was.

"I noticed you were looking at the jeans. They're all handmade. Would you like me to show you the collection?" She proceeded to walk over to the area as she told me a few facts about the designer. She asked if I was from Indianapolis, and I told her I was in town from Washington, D.C. for business. She mentioned she and her husband had lived there for a brief time but ended up in Indianapolis for her husband's career.

"These jeans are our most popular item in the store," she said.

I replied, "Cool buttons" as I casually noticed the price and then exclaimed, "but I'm never going to pay that much for jeans."

"Try them on," she said.

I countered, "I don't care if they feel great. I'm not going to buy them. That's an outrageous price; they're just cotton!"

She persisted with a bit of a laugh, "Try them on. I have clients who have many pairs; they live in these jeans. They're for when you want to dress up a bit with a nice jacket and don't want to wear loose-fitting granny jeans."

I admitted to her that I did want something I could wear for both business and pleasure. But again

I stated firmly, "I didn't come here to buy a pair of jeans."

"Try them on. The fit is everything. What size do you take? They run a bit snug." She picked out a dark stone color in my size. "This color will go with more," she said as she handed them to me to feel. She brought me to the fitting room and said, "I'll be back."

Before I even looked in the mirror, I liked the fit. As I came out, she asked, "Don't they fit well?" I had to agree they did.

"Would you like to see how it looks with this white button-down blouse?"

"Yes."

I put it on. Wow, I'm starting to look good.

"You wear it well," she said. "Would you like to try this embroidered jacket with it?"

"Yes. I love all of it."

"How long are you in town?" she asked.

I replied, "Just until tomorrow. I wish I had more time to meet small business owners here."

Cathy introduced herself by name at that point, only to find out I was the Small Biz Marketing Specialist. We chatted some more as she told me of great small and local businesses in the area to check out before I left. Two minutes later, we were exchanging business cards.

"You pay at the front. How about I give you a brief tour of the Main Street area here?"

I replied, "Absolutely."

A few hours later, I received a personal email thanking me for my purchase along with Cathy's picture and ability to contact her. A few days later, I received a handwritten card with an Indianapolis magnet and coupon code to order online. Very impressive follow-up that made me feel a very strong connection to this small business.

Building toward the Close

Now I know many people could read this as, "Well, what do you expect at a women's boutique?" I can tell you, I expect a lot and most fail miserably... miserably just like the legendary department store.

But here's my point in sharing this story with you: Any small business owner could do the same as Cathy - ***if they wanted to***.

The problem is most don't. If they did, they would look at their sales scripting and make sure they're asking, "Would you like fries with that?" I walked into a business I had never heard of before, wasn't interested in buying anything, yet spent more than I ever would have - and am totally thrilled with my purchase - because the sales person figuratively asked me those six simple words.

As a small business owner, you too can take advantage of this very easy way to increase your profits, all without raising your prices or going out and working hard to find a new customer, client, or patient. The bump, upsell, or cross-sell are ways of expanding the existing purchase of someone who is already in a buying mentality. If the idea of upselling makes you uncomfortable, remember that your goal is never to pressure your customer, client, or patient into unwanted services or to make them spend money irresponsibly. However, remember that it's not the customer's, client's, or patient's job to know everything you do or offer. It's your job to advise them on what additional steps they can take to enhance their purchase and experience, and the bump is a great way to offer them added results.

This is how you can easily put a process in place to ask those six simple words:

Be curious about strangers: Starting from the moment Cathy saw me, she wanted to make a connection.

Why it works: By seeking connection with a stranger, she built rapport long before trying to present the merchandise. This provided her the ability to later insist on me trying on the clothing.

Find a connection: Her simple sharing that she had also lived in Washington, D.C. made her feel familiar to me.

Why it works: We trust people when we discover things in common.

Use analogies: Her image of loose-fitting jeans worn by grandma versus the fit in these made it easy to understand what a fashionable woman's wardrobe shouldn't look like.

Why it works: Painting word pictures with familiar items helps the customer see the benefits, not just hear them.

Don't take no for an answer - in a good way: As much as I said I'd never buy them, she persisted in getting me to the dressing room.

Why it works: 70% of buying decisions are made in the proverbial fitting room. It's a fine line between pushy and determined. Go for determined any day or your "shoppers" never give what you offer the chance to change their lives. Find a way to get them to engage with your product or service. Think about how a car dealership gets you to take a test drive.

Go for the add-on: After I had agreed on the jeans, she suggested a blouse, then a jacket.

Why it works: Once a customer says yes to the main purchase, it is much easier to get them to consider a second.

Also notice….

Too many salespeople work their sales scripting too hard and strive to get the prospect's name as soon as they can, so they can own the shopper.

Cathy didn't get my name until after I had tried on the jeans. She offered hers after she built trust, and building trust is really important to not come off as a used-car salesperson.

In the end, asking, "Would you like fries with that" benefits everyone. Customers get a more satisfying experience, salespeople close larger sales, and companies get more loyal customers and revenue. That's something that's easy to do (and I'm all about making your marketing EZ), so everyone ends up happy.

The 4 R's

There's one final piece to your NURTURE efforts. By focusing on the "N" of the ACTION system, you now have a strong base of loyal customers, clients, or patients. They'd be happy to tell the world about their positive experience - and their WOW! experience - with your company. You just need to ask.

There's four ways to do that. I call it the "4 R's to leverage raving fans":

- Ratings
- Reviews/Testimonials
- Recommendations
- Referrals

It doesn't matter what you say about yourself. What matters is what others say about you. When you're looking for a trustworthy mechanic to fix your car, are you going to just go to the one closest to your home or are you going to ask for recommendations from friends and family, perhaps even asking on social media? When you're looking for a chiropractor to help with that pain you keep getting in your back, are you going to simply look at the chiropractor's website or are you going to see what reviews are available online to learn about others' experiences?

We live in an information-driven economy and everything about you - the good, the bad and the ugly - can easily be found online. Websites such as Google, Facebook, and Yelp are so widely used they have morphed into verbs. Have you ever looked to see what people are saying about your business online? You should. But not just look - that's reactive. Be proactive, and create and implement a plan that actively gets people talking about you - in a good way, of course.

Here are some important stats from the 2017 Local Consumer Review Survey conducted by BrightLocal that show why reputation management is so important:

- 85% of consumers trust online reviews as much as personal recommendations.
- 68% of consumers left a review for a business when asked.
- 49% of consumers need at least a four-star rating before they choose to use a business.

I help my marketing clients with their reputation management. It's a proactive process, meaning we're not sitting and waiting for ratings, reviews, and recommendations to come in. They won't. Well, they won't unless someone is really pissed off. Then that person seems to go out and tell the whole world about it. I want you to have a process in place to proactively get all of the ravings fans you've built by implementing the ACTION system and getting them to be your brand ambassadors.

> When you nurture, you build brand ambassadors, and your existing customers start selling for you!

I encourage my clients to make it a part of their sales process to let prospective customers, clients, or patients know that their having an experience they can't wait to tell everyone about is the #1 priority. You're not going to ask for a rating, review, recommendation, or referral now, but when the time is right, you will. That could be immediately after a meal or three months after working together. The timing depends on the type of solution you're providing.

The easiest way to ask for and get ratings, reviews, recommendations, and referrals is to do it in person. For example, I recently had to buy a new vehicle for my coffee and smoothie business. The sales representative spent a significant amount of time with me, helping me determine the best vehicles in my price range, the different options, and determining which would serve my business needs the best. We got to know each other over the course of that time, talking about the area, our families, and so on. A mini-bond is built in the time spent together.

At the end of the sale, there is now no person better positioned to ask for a review than this sales associate. The associate very nicely asked me if I would be willing to help other customers who are researching their dealership and looking for a true perspective of their business. I really liked how the associate made the referral request about "helping other customers" versus "helping the dealership," although instinctively I know it helps both. I also appreciated that I was offered different ways to review the company. I could get a text, I could get an email, or I could fill out a form right there in the dealership. I requested the text option. An hour after I got home with my new vehicle, I received a text message asking me to leave a review. Of course, I left a positive review and would happily recommend this sales associate and dealership to others. They've nurtured me and are on the path to building a relationship.

Asking customers to leave ratings and reviews of you and your company online is easy. It comes across as a friendly request, and once on a review site, your customer, client, or patient can then either leave a simple rating or can add their own testimonial, sharing more details about why they rated as they did. Most people today understand the importance of reviews, as they use them themselves in making decisions, so most are happy to oblige when asked.

Asking for a referral or recommendation is a bit more of a direct approach of reputation management, and many small business owners shy away from doing it. They tell me, "I don't want to appear desperate or pushy." Or, "It's awkward to ask someone to refer me to their friends and family."

I'm here to help you make that easy and it really is! It's all in how you position it. When a prospective marketing client is thinking of working with me, some will ask me for clients they can speak to for whom I do similar work – a reference.

> The easiest way to get a referral? Deliver a great product or service, then ask!

I actually get these ahead of time, so when I need one, it's easy to reach out. I simply use these words "Would you consider…." After a client has been with me and it's obvious they're seeing positive results from their marketing efforts, I'll send them an email saying, "I have a favor to ask. Would you consider being a referral source for prospective clients wanting to hear from clients like you who have had tremendous success in using our services?"

I've never had one say no. Then when someone wants to speak with them, I send a quick email letting them know some details about the prospective client and the work we'd be doing. They become my brand ambassador, ultimately closing many sales for me as I've had clients tell me, "I had to work with you because 'Client X' just couldn't stop raving about how fabulous your team is and the results they're seeing. I want that for my business. When can we get started?"

Getting referrals is easy when it's positioned as asking your customers, clients, or patients to help connect you to others who are just like them. After all, you've nurtured a great relationship. You want more people just like them. Tell the person that. They'd be flattered and honored.

Here are my top five strategies to help you get started:

- Focus on your "best of the best" customers, clients, or patients. You know who they are. They've probably left five-star reviews for you online. They're actively engaged with you on social media. They're a repeat customer, client, or patient. They know your business so well they could probably work for you. They'd be honored to help your business grow. You just need to ask. That can be as simple as doing it in person or sending an email.

- Help them help you by making it easy to refer. Make it clear exactly who a great referral would be. In my coffee and smoothie business, I share that a great referral is a business with 50 or more employees looking to do something fun and different for staff appreciation events. This helps the referrer winnow down who they know who meets your criteria.
- Provide them with marketing materials they can distribute. This could be anything from a business card, pamphlet, email templates, or referral cards that say, "Referred by __________." This makes it easy for people to refer since they only have to hand out or forward these already-created materials.
- Recognize and thank your referral sources. Let your customers, clients, or patients know how much you appreciate their referrals by calling, emailing, and even better… sending a handwritten note.

- Incentivize. People have good intentions and may say they'll refer you, but everyone enjoys a gift and/or winning something. Incentives such as a gift card, percentage off future work, a small gift, or charitable donation in their name are all powerful for building a lasting bond.

By now, you realize that focusing on keeping the current customers, clients, or patients you have happy keeps your bucket - and bank account - full. You've created WOW! moments, you've built in upsell and cross-sell opportunities, and your raving fans are happy to leave reviews and refer you to others. This is the business you've always dreamed you'd have and by focusing on "N" - NURTURE of the ACTION system, you can now make it a reality.

Get It Done the EZ Way:

- You must take the time to nurture or the other steps you've taken in the ACTION system will lose their traction and benefit to your bottom line.
- It is so much easier and more profitable to keep an existing customer than to find a new one.
- You're sitting on a pot of gold with your existing customers, clients, or patients,

and they are your low-hanging fruit. Take advantage of that.

- NURTURE your existing customers by staying in contact and communicating regularly in ways they'll appreciate.
- It is not your customer's job to remember you. It's your job to stay front-of-mind with them.
- Your business is like a leaky bucket - the water represents your customer base. When you nurture, you plug the leaks to keep more water - customers - in your bucket.
- Create WOW! experiences that make you stand out from your competition and make your customers return for more.
- Six simple words will change your business: "Would you like fries with that?"
- The bump, upsell, or cross-sell are ways of expanding the existing purchase of someone who is already in a buying mentality.
- The 4 R's (ratings, reviews/testimonials, recommendations, and referrals) will go a long way to boosting your business and profitability… but you have to ask for them!

EZ-er Way: Contact The Small Biz Marketing Specialist! smallbizmarketingspecialist.com

Chapter Ten:

Okay, Now What?

You made it this far, congratulations! Seriously, I'm giving you a standing ovation. Most people don't read an entire book. If they even pick up a book at all, they usually browse through it, looking for quick nuggets here or there, then they call it a day.

You're different. You're a smart small business owner who is ready to make their dreams - those dreams you had when you first started your business - a reality. Whatever your motivation is - providing for your family, building a nest egg for retirement, leaving a legacy, etc., you are now holding the blueprint to make those dreams come true.

Perhaps after reading this book, you're ready to pick up the phone to call me, or you're on your keyboard ready to email, "Stacey, please come to my rescue!" (for which I would be happy to take that call or receive that email, and I'll share how to do that at the end).

Hopefully what I've shared resonates with you. It's my passion, my love, and my brilliance to help small business owners with their marketing. It is the ***one*** thing - the ***only*** thing - that will help your business grow, so you can have the dream business you always knew you would.

Remember that I told you at the very beginning that what you're holding is not a book. It's a key – the key to your business success. It's what you do with that key that will either unlock and open the door to your future or keep that door shut and locked forever.

I hate to end with some tough love, but I'm about to get very real with you.

If you're in a predicament and your business isn't where you want it to be right now, there's a reason for it.

There's a reason nine out of ten small businesses fail.

It's not because of lack of capital.

It's not because of lack of skill.

It's not because of lack of ability.

For the most part, everyone has access to the same information. There's this thing called the internet with information on anything and everything you could imagine in different formats such as articles, videos, podcasts, livestreams, and more. You can opt in to receive emails with reports, checklists, ebooks, and more. You can find groups on social media and forums in which people of similar backgrounds hang out. There are books, video training courses, live events, and more. There's no shortage of what you can learn, whether it's this, that, or the other thing. Most of it is free. Some of it has a cost.

The nine out of ten small business owners who fail are those who are always seeking a cure, a remedy, a quick fix - that shiny object - that will miraculously fix everything for them. They jump from one thing to the next, listening to the next charlatan telling them what they want to hear, despite not being able to deliver it.

These nine out of ten small business owners suffer from "I intend syndrome."

- I intend to do marketing.
- I intend to get more customers, clients, or patients.
- I intend to grow sales.
- I intend to be more profitable.

The problem is that "I intend" never happens.

Getting There

What causes the nine out of ten small business owners to fail is one thing: ***Failure to get into action.***

Action is the only thing that will move your business forward. Here's the thing: It doesn't have to be hard (and in this book I've definitely made it "EZ"). Plus it doesn't have to be "all or none."

Have you heard of the law of straight lines? The law of straight lines dictates the shortest path between two points is a straight line. You've probably heard this before. It's one of the basic principles of geometry. It's pretty simple, really. If you want to go to New York from Chicago, you take the simplest and most direct route. You don't go there via Siberia. Similarly, if you want to get a particular result, you don't add any extra steps. You take the simplest and most direct route.

Unfortunately, we tend to add extra steps when we're trying to get something we want. Many times, those extra steps prevent us from getting what we want at all. To demonstrate how the law of straight lines works, I want you to do a little experiment. This may seem a little ridiculous to you at first, but just bear with me. There's a reason to this that will make perfect sense to you shortly.

For this experiment, you'll need a glass of water and a timer, either a watch or a stopwatch. Your target in this experiment is to simply take a sip of water. It's a simple target, but it illustrates a profoundly important point. Now, here we go.

Place the glass of water on the table in front of you. Take out your timer to see which of the following two methods gets you the desired target in the least amount of time. Method number one, the voodoo method. Start your timer. Now look at the glass of water in front of you and keep your attention fixed on it. Close your eyes and say a little prayer for the water. Say, "I ask the universal god force in the sky to manifest this water in my mouth." Sit there for a moment and hope that the universe/God/whatever you believe in will bring the water to you. Take a notice of the result. Now, yell at the water. Say, "Hey, you stupid glass of water, get in my belly." Wait for a moment and see if it complies. Next, tell the water, "I just spent $10,000 on a coaching program that is supposed to make me a millionaire in the next year." See if you have impressed the water enough to make it jump into your mouth.

Now, try sweet talking the water. Say, "Hey, you sexy drink of water, you. Why don't you come up here to my mouth and let me drink ya?" Wait for a moment and see if the water ends up in your mouth. Now try begging the water. Say, "Hey, mister glass of water, can you spare a sip?" Wait for a moment and see if the water has been moved enough to oblige.

Finally, look at the water and think some positive thoughts. Smile at it and feel really confident that the water will wind up in your mouth someday if you think positively about it. Now, stop your stopwatch and take note of the time. Also, take note of the end result. Now, let's try method number two. The straight line.

Start your timer. Pick up the water and take a sip. Set the glass down. Now stop your stopwatch and take a note of the time. Also, take a note of the result. Note the difference in time between these two experiments. Also, note that at the end of method number one… ya didn't have any water in your mouth, did ya? With method number one, you'd ultimately die of thirst. Method number one has the same fatal effect on your business.

This is the simple and obvious power of a straight line. Anything you want in life is subject to the same law. Find the fastest and most direct route and the object of your desire is yours. This seems pretty obvious, right? Why don't we do our marketing like this every day? The problem is you're bombarded with so many distractions every day, the straight line is no longer obvious.

Further, the world is full of charlatans trying to sell you on superstitious thinking, so you've been trained to believe that a number of pointless steps are necessary. We'll talk about how to deal with those problems shortly.

Remember the "O" in the ACTION system?

O is for ongoing. It means doing ***something***… some thing… one thing… right now… each day….

Can you do one thing today that will help your business grow? It doesn't mean you have to sit for eight hours straight without a break until you complete a four-step autoresponder series.

Could you craft the first email in the series today? Could you then craft the second one tomorrow? Could you then test to ensure it looks good on all devices and the links are working?

Here's the thing: If you did one thing to put your marketing into action today, will your business dreams and visions be fulfilled? Of course not. If you don't do one thing to put your marketing into action today, will your business fall apart? Of course not.

I've laid out the ACTION system for you and told you to make it an ongoing part of your business. If I told you that if you would agree to do one thing to market your business every single day, over time, it would be impossible ***not*** to see your business grow and prosper, that those business dreams and visions you have would become reality, if you wanted... ***would you do it?*** On day one, sure. And day two. And maybe day three. But will you still be doing it - taking one step and doing one thing - by the end of the week?

If you kept marketing, over the course of a year, you would have a comprehensive marketing plan, knowing exactly what's working to keep your business growing. You would be attracting the right customers, clients, or patients. You would be connecting with them and helping them through their customer journey, creating mini-transactions along the way. You would be nurturing those connections into relationships to wow, excite, and delight so that people rave about you, coming back again and again with open wallets ultimately becoming brand ambassadors. Would your business have changed? Absolutely. No question. But here, today, because we're in week one, it's an invisible result. You won't necessarily see the results today.

And ***that*** is exactly why most small business owners never achieve their dream business. They do a little bit here, and perhaps a little bit there, but they haven't made marketing an ONGOING part of their business. Don't worry, I'm going to make it easy for you (since that's what this book is all about) to make your marketing ***ongoing***. Because reality is, you have a business to run.

You can do two things right now:

1) You can take the ACTION system and use it as a framework to help your business grow.
   I've given you the actual blueprint of what to do and how to do it. Yes, it's a lot, so I encourage you to go back and re-read it. Highlight the points that you want to remember. Flip down the pages of the end of each chapter to review those key points and answer the questions to formulate your marketing plan. Keep it on your desk as a reference, so you can access it as you're working on creating your marketing efforts.
2) You can take ACTION now to start seeing results sooner rather than later

Look, I know what it's like running a business - I run three of them. I know many small business owners are just too busy to do it on their own. That's why I have a very successful business helping small business owners exactly like you get their marketing into ***action***. Business owners in online businesses and offline businesses. Business owners who are newbies.

Business owners who are 20-year veterans. Business owners in every niche imaginable.

My motto has always been, "Do what you do best and outsource the rest." I hope you've gotten some amazing insights from reading this book. That doesn't mean that you're ready or able to go out and handle every type of marketing your business needs - online, offline, social media (and all the different platforms), email (and the testing required to optimize open and click-thru rates), content marketing (who has the time to write a 1,000 word article, much less repurpose it?), reputation management (reviewing and responding to what people are saying about you on multiple platforms), etc.

Just because you read a book on how to fix your car doesn't mean you can, or should, do it. The best results come when you leave it to the professionals. Same with marketing. Sure, you can definitely do it yourself, and I've laid out the system to help you do it, but that doesn't mean you can, or should.

I'd like to offer you (someone who read the book and who now "gets" marketing but perhaps feels they need help "getting it done") a 30-minute no-obligation consultation with me, "Small Business Stacey."

We'll discuss where you are right now and what your goals are, and I'll make some suggestions for what you can do to achieve them. I'll also share with you what it would be like to work with the Small Business Marketing Specialist should you decide you'd be best served by having marketing experts grow your business.

Here's how to get in touch with me:

(888) 827-8744

info@smallbizmarketingspecialist.com

calendly.com/smallbizstacey

Are you serious about getting what you want or are you someone who just dreams about it?

It's the actions you take that determine whether you get what you want.

What are ***you*** going to do to get into action?

When are you going to do it?

Resources:

Chapter 1 Statistical References:

2017 WASP Barcode Technologies, "State of Small Business Report"

www.waspbarcode.com/about-us/press-release/2017-01-17-small-business-report-2017

Infusionsoft 2017, "Small Business Marketing Trends Report"

www.infusionsoft.com

Street Fight, "Urban Small Business Satisfaction"

http://streetfightmag.com/product/the-urban-smb-report/

Chapter 4

Use this template to help you hone in on and get crystal clear about your avatar and who it is you will best serve with your products and/or services. Remember, specificity matters. The more specific, the better.

CUSTOMER AVATAR WORKSHEET

Who Is He/She

Age #/Age of Children

Marital Status Gender

Location

Sources of Information

Organizations

Publications

Conferences

Gurus

Other

Objections & Opportunities

Role in the purchasing process

Goals & Values

Business Goals

Personal Goals

Challenges & Pain Points

Chapter 8

EZ Marketing Plan Template

The following marketing plan is based on doing a few simple things well. Pick your level of expertise. Do something every day - consistency and persistency are the core tenants of getting your marketing into ACTION.

MARKETING ACTIVITY	BEGINNER	INTERMEDIATE	ADVANCED
Social Media	Pick one platform to focus on	Add additional platforms, leverage each platform's abilities (ex: Facebook groups, Pinterest boards, Twitter social listening), use a scheduling tool	Scale your efforts, run ads, build relationships with influencers
Content Marketing	Keyword research, one original blog post/month	Two blog posts/month, two shared/curated posts, repurpose content	Content calendar with two or more blog posts/month and repurposed into multiple formats
Email Marketing	Lead generation, List building, monthly newsletter	Segmented emails	Automation
Direct Mail	Handwritten notes	Local-focused direct mail	Shock 'n' awe package, integrate with lead generation
Video	Repurpose content with tools such as Lumen4, create videos with images	Share what your business is about via testimonials, case studies, short "how to" videos, staff knowledge/expertise	Webinars, live streams, professional video production

Chapter 9

Small Business Trends
www.smallbiztrends.com

John S. McKean. *Customer's New Voice*. John Wiley & Sons, Inc., Hoboken, New Jersey, 2015

Temkin Group
www.temkingroup.com

Gallo, Amy. "The Value of Keeping the Right Customers." *Harvard Business Review*. 29 Oct. 2014.
https://hbr.org/2014/10/the-value-of-keeping-the-right-customers

BrightLocal: 2017 Local Consumer Review Survey
https://www.brightlocal.com/learn/local-consumer-review-survey/

About the Author

Stacey Riska, aka "Small Business Stacey," is an internationally renowned small business marketing expert and serial entrepreneur. She eats, sleeps, and breathes small business and understands exactly what it takes for the small business owner in any niche or industry to not only survive but to thrive and build the business they dream of.

Her marketing advice indeed "packs a punch" and is based on her own experience pulling one of her entrepreneurial ventures from the brink of collapse (and $500,000 debt) and turning it into a seven-figure profitable business.

With her mantra, "Saving Small Business, Rebuilding Main Street," Stacey's goal is to help 10,000 small businesses achieve success and for each to become a #SmallBizMarketingWiz. To accomplish that goal, Stacey has created Small Biz Marketing Specialist (www.smallbizmarketingspecialist.com) helping small business owners with done-for-you marketing solutions and customized marketing plans. Stacey shares her wisdom and expertise through various services including private coaching, marketing courses, and specialized training programs. She created the Daily Deals for Massive Profits Training Program to teach small business owners how to successfully leverage daily deal sites like Groupon and has also introduced the Silver

Platter Marketing Membership that provides small business owners with ready-to-implement marketing campaigns sent every month.

She's won numerous awards throughout her career for her marketing efforts both in the corporate world prior to launching her own ventures and as a top small business marketing coach. Stacey and her husband live in the Washington D.C. metropolitan area and have two grown children.

Made in the USA
Middletown, DE
16 January 2020

83007152R00109